STUDENT SUCCESS

How To Do Better in College and Still Have Time for Your Friends

THIRD EDITION

Tim Walter
University of Michigan

Al Siebert
Division of Continuing Education,
Portland State University

HOLT, RINEHART AND WINSTON
New York   Chicago   San Francisco   Philadelphia
Montreal   Toronto   London   Sydney
Tokyo   Mexico City   Rio de Janeiro   Madrid

Cover design by Beverly Walter.

Library of Congress Cataloging in Publication Data

Walter, Tim.
  Student success.

  1. Study, Method of.   2. Success.   I. Siebert, Al.   II. Title.
LB2395.W35   1984   378′.1702812   83-22544

ISBN 0-03-063676-0

CBS COLLEGE PUBLISHING
Holt, Rinehart and Winston
The Dryden Press
Saunders College Publishing

About this Book ...

Student Success is a unique book that was created in an unusual way. During the early 1970s, our friend Jim McConnell asked us to write a student manual to accompany his new introductory psychology textbook, *Understanding Human Behavior.* Jim made two requests. He asked us to write a student manual that would provide students with practical tips on how to make learning both more efficient and more rewarding. He also asked us to show students how to study in ways that would make it possible to retain what they had learned for years to come.

Our response to these requests was to begin the student manual with a section on learning and study skills. The section was titled "How To Do Better in College and Still Have Time for Your Friends."

The student manual was published in March 1974. Before we knew what had happened, our publisher started receiving telephone calls and letters from college administrators, orientation directors, and instructors asking for permission to duplicate "How To Do Better in College and Still Have Time for Your Friends." From across the country requests came in. Administrators and instructors wanted to distribute the section to all the students in a department, to the incoming freshman class, or, in the case of one university president, to the entire student body of some 18,000 students!

Our editor was pleased with the positive response and surprised us by asking us to write a book on "How To Do Better in College and Still Have Time for Your Friends." She asked us to include all the things that we as psychologists knew were related to succeeding in college. Her request resulted in the first edition of *Student Success* in 1976.

In *Student Success* you will find the best information available on doing well in college. The book is organized into three parts:

Part One: Getting Oriented and Motivated for Success in College

> *Habits, attitudes, and self-motivation:* How to increase your chances of graduating by being self-motivated and developing habits and attitudes that lead to success in college and success in life.
>
> *Using all the support services on campus:* How to benefit from all the campus resources available to you.

Part Two: Doing Well in Classes

Time management: How to develop a study schedule that keeps you from studying too much, provides enough study time for you to accomplish your study goals, and reserves ample time for athletics, music, social life, work, important causes, or other interests.

Specific study skills: The best ways to take notes, study for tests, write papers, and pass tests.

Part Three: Doing Well in School and Life

Working with instructors: Getting the most out of every course by working with instructors rather than being misled by common myths about instructors.

Teaching styles and learning styles: What to do when you don't have a good match between your learning style and an instructor's teaching style.

Building good friendships: Lack of friends is a major distraction for some students. *Student Success* devotes a chapter to friendships.

Self-actualization: How to use college experiences as a starting point for lifelong self-development.

Student Success does more than just provide useful information, however. One of its strengths is that at the end of each chapter you will find Action Projects and Checklists, which are designed to help you organize your efforts to benefit from the material in the chapter. Whether you are taking a college orientation course, a study skills course, have been assigned the book by an instructor, or have simply picked up *Student Success* at your bookstore, you will find a wealth of practical suggestions. By using *Student Success*, your adjustment to college will be a more pleasurable experience. Your learning will be more enjoyable and permanent. You will have a better chance of reaching your goal of graduating with a good education.

Tim Walter
Al Siebert

How To Use this Book

First, take a minute to skim through this book. Read the questions that precede each chapter to develop a feel for what you will learn. Also ask yourself questions that you will want answered as you read the book. Do that now.

If you usually ask questions as you skim material, that's great! You have an active mind and quickly grasp the main ideas in written material. But if you tend to glance through books without asking questions, that is a sign that you need to improve your reading skills. Learning to ask questions is one of the first habits that you may want to work on.

Here are some questions that might be asked while skimming through the book:

What must I do to be successful?
How can studying be easier?
Can I improve my intelligence?
What are some tips on how to do better on exams?
How can I write better papers more rapidly without making them longer?
Why is there a whole chapter on study goals?
What do successful students do?
How can I enjoy courses taught by instructors I dislike?
How can I have more good friends?
What does it mean to view life as a school?
Who can help me when I need help to succeed?

Second, don't think you have to do everything all at once! Pick several skill areas that you believe will be the most helpful to you and try them first. Skip sections that you don't want to use yet.

This book is a compilation of many practical tips and psychological principles. It can take a long time to learn how to use them all. The key to the successful use of the book is not to try to do it all, at least not at the start. You'll burn yourself out. Try a few things until they become habits, and then work on building a few more habits. This is a book you will want to keep and review every few months.

Remember that habits take time to acquire. Habits take months to develop, but once you have them, you have them for life!

CONTENTS

PART ONE

Getting Oriented and Motivated for Success in College

Chapter 1

Taking Responsibility for Being Successful

Are you entering college intending to graduate?

Can you name the two most important factors that determine whether or not a student will graduate?

Do you understand the difference between "either/or" thinking and "both/and" thinking?

How would you define success?

How much do you feel responsible for your successes and failures?

Did you know that the way you daydream affects your future?

Have you discovered how to motivate yourself with self-chosen goals?

Having It Both Ways

Only 40% of the students in your freshman class will still be with the class when it graduates. About 20% will "stop out" for a while but will eventually get their degrees. The other 40% will never receive degrees. Nationwide, that is what the statistics show.

Can you guess what the two most important factors are that will determine whether or not you will still be with your class when it graduates?

I.Q. is not one of them. The two most important determining factors are having a self-motivated desire to get a good education and having good learning skills.

These two factors, motivation and learning skills, are interrelated. Many students know how to study and learn, but they lack the motivation to do so. Some students are strongly motivated to succeed, but because of poor learning skills and bad study habits they waste a lot of time and energy. They make school hard work instead of an enjoyable experience and tend to burn themselves out.

If you listen to what students say about their attitudes toward college, you will discover that a number of students have an "either/or" mind set about college. They believe that the only two choices available are *either* to be a bookworm, grinding away at the books all the time, *or* to enjoy the good life, doing barely enough schoolwork to maintain a C average.

Our purpose in writing *Student Success* is to show you how it is possible to have a "third choice." You can *both* enjoy your college years to the fullest *and* graduate with an excellent education.

Student Success is organized in three parts to help you see how to make use of your third choice. Part One focuses on motivation and attitudes toward college. Part Two covers all aspects of learning how to learn and be successful in your classes in a way that leaves you with time for friends, work, athletics, or other important activities. Part Three integrates dealing with the challenges in college as practice for dealing successfully with challenges in life.

Accept Total Responsibility for Learning

In college, consider adopting the philosophy that your instructors are responsible for no more than presenting ideas and information to you. Assume it is your responsibility to learn. Too often students are conditioned by magazines, television, and movies to be *passive*. Students expect to be entertained by textbooks and instructors. The only writings or instructors these students pay attention to are those that catch their attention. These students seem to expect instructors to compete for their attention just as professional entertainers do.

College instructors are not encouraged to become entertainers. Being an entertainer in the classroom is viewed as unprofessional at most schools. How much time and money do you think your instructors are given to prepare jokes, write funny lines, create witty sayings, come up with humorous comments, and do all the other preparation that Richard Pryor and Lily Tomlin go through? None at all.

You will be very fortunate to find an occasional instructor who not only knows the material completely but can add wit and charm to the presentation. Most instructors have much information to present to you for your consideration. Ask no more of your instructors. Instructors are simply not in the entertainment business. In fact, to become a college instructor there are no requirements to take even one course in public speaking or public presentation. If you find an instructor who is an excellent speaker and skilled at presenting information to a large audience, you most likely have an unusual instructor rather than a typical one.

Consider developing the attitude that you are going to be an *active learner*. You are going to get the most out of every class. You have paid your money, so get what you've paid for. You are the consumer! You can even make a boring class interesting by assuming that every instructor has useful information for you. Be determined to learn everything you can from your instructors and textbooks.

REMEMBER: The best investment you will ever make is in yourself. You may lose your job or money, but no one can take your education away from you!

Be Responsible for Your Successes and Failures

Being responsible for yourself means taking credit for your successes and for your failures as well. Are you a person who feels responsible for the way your life goes? Do you take credit for your successes? For your failures?

Successful students feel responsible for themselves. People having trouble in college tend to dismiss success as "good luck" and blame others for their woes. Perhaps you've heard students say,

"I could get to class on time if it weren't for _____!"
"She gave me an 'A' on my paper. I really lucked out."
"How can you enjoy going to a class taught by a guy who _____?"
"Nobody at this college cares about students. There's no way we can do well here."
"I would have gotten that job if it hadn't been for . . . ."

Such statements are made by people who don't feel responsible for what happens in their lives. They don't see the relationship between what they do and the results they get.

To do better in college, make your success or failure your responsibility. Say to yourself, "My success is my responsibility. It is not dependent upon instructors, employers, relatives, friends, classmates, administrators, rules, regulations, or fate. I get credit for my successes! I am responsible for my successes and failures."

Practice saying such positive statements as the following and notice the effect they have on you:

"If I use good study techniques, I will earn good grades."
"I will do well in this class by paying close attention to the instructor."
"My grades depend on my effort, not luck."
"People will care more about me when I care more about them."

Define Success with Goals

Consider defining success as: "Success is reaching my goals." Using this definition as a basis, what is the first step necessary for you to experience being successful? That's right, it means you must first set a goal!

People who rarely set goals for themselves rarely experience being successful. People who don't set goals are neither successful nor unsuccessful. They are *not* successful.

A person without goals may never have thought of setting goals. Other people don't set goals for themselves because the possibility of not reaching the goals is risky. They fear failure. They try to avoid feelings of failure by not setting goals.

Sometimes people try to avoid feelings of failure by setting impossibly high goals. Perhaps you can remember hearing a student with very low grades announce at the start of the school year that he or she was going to get a straight A average this time. You know what happens next. The student falls short of an A on the first few tests and papers and shrugs off lower grades without feeling failure. The goal of going from a 1.9 GPA to a 4.0 GPA in one jump has such a low probability of being reached that the person has a built-in excuse for not reaching it. Thus no feelings of failure are experienced.

Psychologists understand the dynamics and processes of success and failure very well. Psychologist David McClelland spent many years studying those individuals who are good at setting and achieving goals. He developed a way of testing college students that accurately predicts which ones will achieve the most career success. McClelland finds that the best predictor of your future is your fantasy life. *Whatever you dwell on in your mind in a relaxed state tends to be a blueprint for your future!*

6

Four Fantasy Components
Related to Goal Achievement

McClelland measures achievement motivation by asking people to tell imaginative stories to pictures that they are shown. Then the stories are examined for these four features:

1. The fictional person is working to achieve a goal, to do something better or to accomplish something that others have not.
2. The person in the story has a strong need and an emotional desire to reach the goal.
3. Reaching the goal will not be easy because of certain blocks, handicaps, or barriers, which are carefully considered and examined.
4. The person in the story keeps searching for ways to reach the goal, may get help from others, but the main reason the goal is reached is because of effort.

If your thoughts or expectations about school don't have the four components described above, that's all right. The mental activities related to being more successful are habits that can be learned.

Daydream about Being Successful

To increase your chances of achievement spend time visualizing being successful. See places and scenes. Picture yourself there as though watching a television program. Use your imagination to carry on possible conversations.

Once you've chosen a goal for yourself, spend time visualizing yourself as having achieved it. Daydream about how people would talk to you. Imagine what positive things people will say. Visualize the pleasant reactions of instructors and employers and others who may have contact with you. See yourself walking, speaking, feeling, and talking after achieving success. Involve all the senses you can. Imagine yourself being treated to a movie or concert by someone who is impressed with your accomplishments.

Prepare for Difficulties

Anticipate possible difficulties and see yourself successfully coping with them. Mentally rehearse good outcomes again and again.

"Doesn't attention to the possible blocks and barriers mean that you have a negative attitude?" Not at all. When a person motivated by goals is determined to have things work out well, he or she tries to anticipate all possible difficulties and find ways to work around them.

A person motivated to achieve goals does not have a negative attitude; he or she is being practical and realistic. A person who says

"There won't be any problems; I don't want to talk about them" is naive. A naive optimist will undertake projects without pausing to think about the possibility of difficulties arising. A person with a desire to achieve is both optimistic about the outcome and realistic about the negative factors involved in achieving goals.

A realistic positive attitude includes being able to look at the problems, the difficulties, the negative factors which have to be coped with. Take a moment now to answer this question: "By choosing to do well in school, what are some of the problems and difficulties that I have to cope with?"

Here are some of the negative factors reported to us by good students:

It takes more energy.
You work harder than poor students.
Risk of failure.
Less time for friends.
Less chance to loaf around.
You miss some fun things because of studying for assignments or tests.
People expect more ("you get a B and they have a heart attack!").
Inability to go out for sports as often because practice interferes with studying.
Greater likelihood of being "razzed" and called "bookworm" or "egghead."
Family is upset because you don't have as much time for them.
People give you a bad time if your grades drop a little.
Some people think you're weird if you get top grades.

To this list of negative factors we would add:

Exposure to too much information too fast.
Delayed payoff for learning. The real benefits are far away and not definite. Grades are temporary motivators and are not the end goal.
Required courses of uncertain value.
Not enough sleep because of having to study late at night.

Perhaps as you've read these various sources of negative stress you've come up with several more of your own. There are many forces working against you, and that's exactly why we've included these lists. If it were easy to be successful, more students would be.

So, what can be done?

If you make yourself aware of all the forces working against you, you will be better prepared to hold up against them. You will avoid "burnout."

Set Goals to Motivate Yourself

Self-chosen goals are motivating forces. Once you establish the goals you want to accomplish, your goals give you direction. You provide an instant frame of reference for deciding what to do or not to do. When you do something that helps you move closer to your goals, your brain will say, "That's right, go ahead, that's just what you want to do, that's good!"

If you don't have goals, your brain will be in a quandary. Your brain might say, "I guess that's good. Wait a minute, I'm not sure, I really can't say. What do others think? I don't know. I'm not sure what to do. Let's wait and see what happens."

A person without goals is like a ball in a pinball machine, bouncing back and forth from bumper to bumper, gradually allowing the force of gravity to determine where it ends up. Having goals is like planning a vacation trip. You know your destination. By setting goals you don't wander in a meaningless direction. Remember, however, that it is all right and quite normal to start college without definite life goals.

Many students lack clearly defined and well-thought-out goals. For many students, especially those in orientation programs, a main purpose of college is to choose some goals and determine how they might best be achieved.

Setting goals has a naturally motivating effect. Once you have that feeling of direction, that desire to achieve a goal, you'll need some added support. As you work toward your goals, you'll need to give yourself those pats on the back. Every time you study for an hour, consider rewarding yourself with a break. If you do well on a quiz, consider a reward such as relaxing with your favorite reading or a television program. By planning to reward yourself, you'll constantly be aware that at the end of all that work is a well-deserved payoff.

Build Self-Confidence Gradually

"How can I be sure that I will achieve my goals?" The way to build confidence in yourself is to set moderately challenging goals. We emphasize throughout the book, *only* set goals that you truly believe you can reach, using reasonable effort. Then when you reach the goal, this gives you a good experience of yourself. Your self-confidence increases, and the next time you set a slightly more challenging goal.

Set Course Goals

Take a moment right now to practice specifying some definite short-term goals for yourself and to select some possible ways of rewarding yourself for reaching those goals.

Directions: List the courses you are taking. Set one goal for each course that you would like to accomplish within the next week, month, and semester.

Courses	One-Week Goal	One-Month Goal	Semester Goal

Now that you have set your goals, ask yourself, "How could I reward myself if I accomplished each goal? List the rewards you could give yourself if you accomplished your weekly, monthly, and semester goals.

Rewards: 1.
             2.
             3.
             4.

Develop Your Career Goals and Life Goals

Do You Have Some Clearly Specified Long-Range Goals for Yourself? Deciding what you want out of life and going after it can be a very strong motivating force in your life. By setting goals you give yourself purpose. There is no use being lost in the wilderness. Goals help you cut a clear path through the underbrush to the destination that you aim for.

Later on, we are going to show you in detail how to go about setting and achieving specific study goals. Right now, we ask you to focus on personal goals, on life goals. We ask you to dream a little and contemplate your college career and life in general.

Think back to those years in grade school. Do you remember the teacher or relative who thought it was a good thing to ask children, "What do you want to be when you grow up?" If you were influenced by television, movies, and storybooks, as most of us were, and understood that answering this question was part of the game you had to play, you probably said things like doctor, nurse, astronaut, or someone like a television hero who popped into mind.

The reality of career goal setting is that most people who graduate from high school don't really know what they want to be. In fact, many college students don't know what they want to do after graduation. There is a better plan of attack than just seeing what careers are available about the time you graduate.

If you've entered college without a specific career, you needn't get in a tizzy. A tizzy won't help you or anyone around you. Instead, think about what you want to be and where you want to go in life. You have plenty of time to make career choices. In fact, most people make four major career changes during their lives.

One resource available to you is at the office or center that provides career counseling. The counselors can provide you with aptitude and interest tests which correlate your particular interests and inclinations with certain careers. The best thing you can do to assess career opportunities is to observe and talk to people in various occupations.

We have spent a lot of time watching and talking to happy and unhappy college students. Some students know how to motivate themselves. Others sit around griping and complaining about how unmotivated they are. If you talk to motivated students you will find that they motivate themselves by choosing and pursuing goals during their college years. In choosing goals for college, most successful students ask themselves a series of questions like these:

> "What would I enjoy doing that would be worthwhile for me to do?"
> "What knowledge, skill, or ability can I acquire that I will enjoy and that will provide me with income?"
> "What sort of person do I want to be when I leave college?"
> "What courses and experiences will help me develop into the person I would like to be?"
> "What interests, hobbies, or abilities do I now have that could be turned into an enjoyable occupation?"

If nothing specific is ahead of you now, then consider setting as a goal discovering what goals you'd like to have. Here's a clue to look for. A well-chosen goal:

> excites you; you can hardly wait to get started.
> is definite and specific; you know exactly what it is you're aiming for.
> is specific and measurable; you will be able to see and evaluate your progress.
> fits you well; it enables you to mesh your interests, personality, and skills.
> is challenging; it isn't easy to reach, but it is reasonable and achievable in the amount of time available.
> will be personally satisfying to reach, regardless of what others may think.

People who live fulfilling lives are often future oriented. Ask around, talk to people who seem to be living life to the fullest, people who are truly enjoying themselves. We'll bet that most people you talk to of

11

this nature are people who have in mind some future accomplish-ments. These are people who are oriented toward having something work better, toward learning a new skill, or toward accomplishing something that will be satisfying and rewarding.

There is nothing wrong with living for the present. But to increase the likelihood of more pleasant future moments, plan ahead and take action. You can both enjoy life now and work toward a good future.

Action Project: Career Goal Setting

Directions: Keeping in mind the six characteristics of a well-chosen goal, in the space below write in some goals that fit into your career plans. Describe goals that would be fun to accomplish by the end of your first school year, the second year, and by graduation.

One-Year Goal: _____

_____

Two-Year Goal: _____

_____

Graduation Goal: _____

_____

© 1967 United Feature Syndicate, Inc.

Action Project: Increasing Your Chances of Graduating With Your Class

To apply the knowledge about the ways of thinking that lead to success, spend some time reflecting on the following questions:

1. ___ ___ ___ Why am I in college? Because everyone else is? Because most of my high school friends came to college? Because my parents always told me that I would go to college? Have I chosen to be here because I want to be?

2. ___ ___ ___ How much do I really want to become an educated person? Am I here to become educated, to obtain a college degree, or what? How much do I truly desire an education? In my imagination can I actually see myself graduating?

3. ___ ___ ___ What are all the difficulties I face? What percentage of students entering here actually graduate? What might prevent me from getting my education?

4. ___ ___ ___ What resources are available to me? What sort of help is there to assist me in getting past difficulties that I might encounter?

Chapter 2

Differences in Attitudes Between Successful and Unsuccessful Students

Do you understand the role of attitudes in determining success in school?

Did you know that there are wide differences among people in their beliefs about how much their lives are controlled by external forces and fate?

Have you ever realized that attitudes are habits that are learned?

Have you ever observed that too much freedom can be a problem for some people?

Can you list some advantages to having a negative attitude?

Did you realize that achievement imaging requires both positive and negative thinking?

Did you know that there are some typical games students play that work contrary to doing well in school?

Do you know the steps to follow to develop more positive attitudes?

Attitudes Can Help or Hinder

Attitudes are mental and emotional habits. Like all habits, they are learned. Also, like other habits, they occur without conscious effort. Because they are learned, you can do something about counterproductive attitudes that work against you reaching your goals.

Knowledge that success comes from setting and reaching goals can be helped or hindered by attitudes. Many students have attitudes which prevent them from being successful and accepting responsibility for what happens to them.

A few students devote so much mental activity to finding fault with teachers and school they have little time or energy left over for doing the things that lead to useful learning. Many students have negative attitudes about certain subjects. They believe they can't do well in math or music, for example, and as a result do not even try to do well.

Some students won't think negative thoughts about anything. They will not think about potential problems or difficulties because they are conditioned to avoid negative thinking.

The most difficult problem for most students entering college is having too much freedom. Throughout high school their lives were organized, controlled, and structured by external forces. They have developed an attitude of expecting to be told whatever they need to know. They don't relate well to all this talk about setting and reaching self-chosen goals.

An Attitude Checkup

Before continuing with the subject of attitudes, let's do a quick check to find out your attitude toward the idea that you can do something about how well your life goes for you. Take several minutes right now to look at the pairs of statements on the following page. Put a check mark by the statement in each pair that, in general, is closest to what you believe is true. Even if there is some truth to both statements, go ahead and select the one that is more true than the other.

15

1. ____ Promotions are earned through hard work and persistence.

____ Promotions usually come from having the right people like you.

2. ____ I would get better grades if the teaching in this school were better.

____ How hard I study determines the grades I get.

3. ____ The increasing divorce rate indicates that fewer people are trying to make their marriages last.

____ Fate determines how long a marriage will last. All you can do is hope your partner will stay with you for life.

4. ____ It is useless to try to change another person's opinions or attitudes.

____ When I want to, I can usually get others to see things my way.

5. ____ In our society a person's income is determined largely by ability.

____ Finding a well-paying job is a matter of being luckier than the next guy.

6. ____ I have very little ability to influence people.

____ If I handle people right, I can usually influence them.

7. ____ My grades are a result of my effort; luck has little to do with it.

____ Whether I study or not has little effect on the grades I get.

8. ____ It is wishful thinking to believe that one can influence what happens in society at large.

____ People like me can change the course of world events by making ourselves heard.

9. ____ I am the master of my fate.

____ When I see an unfortunate person, I sometimes think "There but for the grace of God go I."

10. ____ Many people are difficult to get along with, and there is no use trying to be friendly.

____ Getting along with people is a skill that can be learned.

11. ____ I am usually a good influence on others.

____ Running around with bad company leads a person into bad ways.

12. ____ I would be much happier if people weren't so irritating.

____ Peace of mind comes from learning how to adapt to life's stresses.

*To score yourself, add up the number of check marks you have for odd-numbered items on the left-hand side and even-numbered items on the right. Count up the check marks you have for the following: left side, items 1, 3, 5, 7, 9, 11; right side, items 2, 4, 6, 8, 10, 12.

Controlling Your Life

The higher your score on this attitude survey, the more you probably feel that you have control over how well your life goes. Students who know they are personally responsible for many of the successes and failures that occur in their lives are called "high internals" by some social scientists. Such students believe that what controls the important forces and experiences in their lives is inside themselves.

Students with low scores believe that they are the helpless pawns of fate. They believe that forces influencing their lives are external to themselves. These students are called "high externals."

The point we want to make here is that both sets of attitudes are correct. Each of these attitudes is self-maintaining. Students who are high internals believe they can influence much of what happens to them. They take actions to make things happen. The results of their efforts confirm their beliefs. Students who are high externals seldom take action. They believe it won't do any good. Sure enough, most of what happens to them is determined by outside forces and other people.

The fact that you are reading this book is an indication that you are probably a person who is "internal." You know that a book such as this can provide some practical tips on how to be more effective. People who are high "externals" respond to a book like this by saying, "It won't do me any good." They are right. Their habitual way of responding to learning opportunities and chances for personal growth maintains their attitude that it doesn't do any good to try.

How To Replace Negative Thinking with Practical Optimism

Can a person change? Can a person develop attitudes and thinking habits different from what they now have?

Yes.

The first step toward developing more positive attitudes is to recognize the difference between positive and negative.

People with positive attitudes tend to:

look for the good in a situation.
be optimistic about outcomes.
be happy about whatever good things are happening.
be pleasant people to be around.
be rarely sidetracked by irritations.
focus on getting good results.
believe that a positive expectation can improve a negative situation.

People with negative attitudes tend to:

find something wrong in any situation.
be pessimistic about outcomes.

be unhappy because some good things have not happened.

believe things will eventually get worse.

be unpleasant to be around.

be easily distracted by irritations.

focus on having good intentions.

believe that their negative attitudes are a legitimate consequence of a negative situation.

Advantages to Being Negative

We want to caution you, however, about having a negative attitude toward people with negative attitudes. For one thing, people with negative attitudes make people with positive attitudes look good. They are useful to have around. And there are many advantages to having a negative attitude. If there weren't any advantages, no one would stay negative very long!

Some advantages of a negative attitude are

you can frustrate people who would like to influence you.

people don't expect as much of you.

you get more attention.

the world is more predictable.

it's easier than being positive.

you avoid disappointment.

you avoid responsibility for things that go wrong.

you have fun playing games with people.

Finding Value in Both Positive and Negative Thinking

Once you realize that there are some advantages to negative thinking you can use them to counterbalance the disadvantages that come from chronic optimism. Now you can more skillfully do with your imagination what McClelland described as leading to achievement. You can look with optimism toward a possible accomplishment and increase your chances of success by anticipating and avoiding various things that could go wrong.

How can you tell if you have a negative attitude? If you don't know, then you probably tend to be negative. People with positive attitudes usually know that they have them. A person maintains a positive attitude pretty much out of choice. He or she is consciously aware of the existence of the attitude and how useful it is to maintain it. People who are in the middle (neither strongly positive nor strongly negative) or who tend to be negative usually have not thought much about their attitudes, and certainly they haven't considered that they have a choice about the attitudes they hold.

Consistent with what we've said about "high externals," people with negative attitudes rarely entertain the idea that they can do anything about the attitudes they have. As one rather negative student said, "An attitude is an attitude and you're stuck with what you've got."

Attitude Differences

When we originally passed out some drafts of this book for review, a student with a positive attitude said, "Hey! Good! Maybe I can get more tips on how to do better in chemistry." A student with a negative attitude said, "Well, I can try some of these things, but they probably won't work for me."

Positive people tend to look for ways to improve. There is the desire to be better and an awareness that people can learn how to be better. Negative people aren't oriented toward learning and improvement. If urged to do something by external forces (other people pressuring them), they may promise to "try." But the promise "I'll try" usually signifies that they will only go through the motions for a while. They expect to eventually drift back into acting as they always have.

Another key difference in attitude is whether or not you learn from experience. A person with a positive attitude has a positive attitude toward mistakes. As one scientist wrote, "If your experiment goes exactly as predicted, you don't learn anything. The times when you learn something are those times when your experiment does not go as predicted."

A person with a positive attitude is unhappy about making a mistake or not reaching a goal, but this person starts thinking, "What will I do the next time this happens?" Examples of positive thinking are:

"The next time I'm asked a question like that . . . ."
"The next time she says that to me, I'm going to say . . . ."
"The next time I'm in a situation like this, here's what I'm going to do . . . ."

The positive person tends to focus on the future; the negative person tends to dwell on the past. This person spends a lot of time feeling sorry for what has happened.

"I would be able to study if I didn't have such a gabby roommate."
"I probably could do better in English if my high school teacher had taught me something."
"I thought I would like psychology, but the instructor bores me to death."

Do you recognize any of these mental habits in yourself? If you recognize some of the negative statements as similar to ones you make, we hope you've also recognized by now that you have a choice about how you allow your mind to react. All these reactions are *learned.* Successful people work at acquiring positive mental habits.

We don't want to mislead you into thinking that a person has to change his or her attitudes before performance will improve. There is ample evidence to show that the opposite is often true. After first changing performance, a person can find that the attitude has changed. William James was one of the first to discover that changing attitudes can change behavior and that changing behavior can change attitudes. This is partly why we often recommend in our book that even though you're not quite sure that something will work, you should go ahead and act as though it will work. In many instances, we will encourage you to act as successful students do. Frequently, you will find that when you begin acting as an effective and skillful person does, your attitudes and expectations will soon fall into line with your behavior.

Avoid Games Losers Play

It is all right to feel sorry for yourself once in a while, but if you do it frequently, you may be playing a game. A game, as explained by Eric Berne, occurs when a person follows a sequence of actions or words that manipulates others into responses that provide a hidden psychological payoff. The game is not usually fun or pleasant. The moves are superficially plausible, but the real motive is hidden. Game playing is like "conning" someone but differs in that a "con" is conscious, whereas game playing usually goes on without conscious awareness.

Keep in mind that playing games is not a sign that someone is "sick." We just want to show that the games students play often have payoffs that prevent them from being successful in school. It may be that you play some games that hinder your ability to do well in school.

YES, BUT . . . .

A good example to start with is the game "Yes, but . . . ." It was the first game that Eric Berne analyzed, and it led to his development of transactional analysis.

Student: "I can't seem to concentrate."
"You could study in your room, instead of in the cafeteria."
"Yes, but it's too noisy there."
"Why don't you shut your door and play your radio?"
"Yes, but my roommate always talks to me."
"Why don't you . . . ."
"Yes, but . . . ."
On the surface, the student seems to be asking for suggestions about how to keep from being distracted. The real purpose of the in-

teraction, however, is to prove to others that nothing they suggest is going to work.

AIN'T IT AWFUL . . . ?

Minimartyr is walking down the hall after class and, as usual, starts a conversation by saying,

> "Ain't it awful the way she loads work on us?"
> ". . . the way she grades?"
> ". . . how the tests are written?"
> ". . . how the lectures are so boring?"
> ". . . the way we have to sit on those hard seats?"

WOODEN LEG

"How can anyone expect me to do well with the troubles I have. If you had the problems I have—my family and I get into these big arguments each week and I have these headaches; I lost all my notes; I can't sleep at night; I'm broke . . . ."
"I know someone who has lots of the same problems."
"My problems are worse! No one has problems as bad as mine."

HARRIED

Whirlwind takes on everything and volunteers for more. A moving dynamo of activity, Whirlwind works frantically on dozens of projects. On the verge of exhaustion, he or she charges ahead. There are meetings to attend, phone calls to make, people to see, details to arrange.
"Studying? Have to put that off until later."
Whirlwind is busy but doesn't get much accomplished.

REMEMBER: The more goals you have, the less likely you are to reach any of them.

STUPID

"Oh no! There I go again. Look how dumb I am! I always do these *stupid* things. I always find some way to foul things up! I always make some dumb mistake."
True.

IF IT WEREN'T FOR HIM . . . .

"I could get good grades in math if it weren't for the instructor."
"I would have a good grade average if it weren't for my counselor making me take those tough courses."

"I would go to class if the instructor weren't so boring."

"I could have qualified for a scholarship if the instructor hadn't given me a C in biology."

"I could study better if it weren't for the noise at home."

Pay Attention to Repeating Problems

These games all have predictable patterns, and they are repeated. The same thing happens again and again and again. The person doesn't change or find a way to deal with what happens. The gains from game playing seem to be worth more than whatever costs there may be, including being not successful as a student.

There are more games that people play. There are even games played by students who get top grades. By mentioning a few games that scholastic losers play, we have tried to show that students who would like to be more successful may unknowingly act in ways that work contrary to their chances of being successful.

Blaming others for your failures is a surefire way to avoid knowing yourself and avoid learning useful lessons about life. People who blame others for their difficulties are usually not successful. Their theme song is "If only other people would change, my world would be a better place for me." You needn't fall into these traps. By following the suggestions outlined in *Student Success* you can have more success if you really want it.

Action Project: Habit and Attitude Assessment

Now that we have talked about habits and attitudes, take a minute to list the habits and attitudes you have that you believe might be helping or hindering your academic and personal development. For suggestions on the habits and attitudes that *Student Success* might help you develop, look through the entire book.

List Some Useful Habits and Attitudes You Now Have:
1.
2.
3.
4.
5.

List Some Harmful Habits and Attitudes You Now Have:
1.
2.
3.
4.
5.

List Some Habits and Attitudes *Student Success* Might Help You
Develop:
1.
2.
3.
4.
5.

Self-Development Project: Gaining a More Positive Attitude about School

Keeping in mind that attitudes are habits, take a moment to answer
this question: "If I really wanted to, could I acquire a new habit or
change an old one?" Most people feel that they would be able to
change a habit or acquire a new one if they truly wanted to. We recognize, however, how important it is that any effort to develop a new
habit *must be self-chosen!* This means that all of our suggestions
about developing useful habits are just that—only suggestions. Having worked with many hundreds of students at improving their ability to get the most out of their educational experiences, we know that
no one succeeds at developing new habits when ordered to do so. So
keep in mind that any time we suggest a useful habit, take a while to
decide whether or not it is a habit that you truly feel would benefit
you.

Many of the students who show up at the centers for improving
study skills have negative attitudes. They are negative about going to
school, about attending classes, about teachers, and about studying.
Being a person who sincerely wants to get a better education, who
works at improving attitudes about school, classes, and study, is as
important as learning effective studying techniques. Here is a four-
week plan for gaining a more positive attitude, which has been used
successfully with many hundreds of students.

Step 1: Take several days to make up a list of the negative
thoughts, feelings, and statements that occur from the
time you wake up in the morning until the time you go to
sleep at night. To develop a complete list, it is useful to
carry a small notebook or some blank 3×5 cards to write
down thoughts, statements, or feelings immediately after
they occur. **NOTE:** It is important that you do not criticize
yourself for having negative thoughts or statements. First,
we want to get an accurate picture of what exists.

Step 2: Using the same method, write down the thoughts, feelings,
and statements of a positive nature that occur for several
days. This step is at the information-gathering stage, so do

23

not yet try to emphasize or increase the number of positive thoughts or statements. Our objective here is to gain information about how frequently they occur at the present time.

Step 3: Each day for the next 28 days have your cards or notebook with you. As you go through the day, record each time that you say or think something that is a sign of having a positive attitude. Record this as it occurs. At the same time, keep a record of any negative thoughts, feelings, or statements that you make. During this four-week period, if you find that a negative thought or statement has occurred, then try to follow it or replace it with a more positive statement.

Step 4: Each night, record on a chart the number of positive feelings and statements that occurred during the day and the number of negative feelings or statements that occurred. This program will help you become more aware (a) of your own thoughts, feelings, and statements and (b) of the fact that you can choose to increase or decrease thoughts, feelings, and statements which you make. Students using this program have been able to significantly increase their positive attitudes toward school, classes, and studying and have been able to decrease their negative reactions. **NOTE:** As you go through the program, you will find more statements and thoughts occurring to add to your original lists, so feel free to revise them as you go along.

Chapter 3

Your College Resources

Did you ever stop to think that every office and service at the college exists to help you get the education you desire?

Have you realized that as a student your curiosity is welcomed by people who work for the college?

Did you know that the college has many ways to assist you in getting financial aid if you need it?

Could you list for a classmate the wide variety of resources available to students?

Be Assertive, Curious, and Snoopy

Students who feel personally responsible for doing well in college seek information. They explore the college asking questions. They go beyond whatever is covered in the "orientation" program or course. One of the best ways to measure your own sense of self-responsibility is to notice how active you are at familiarizing yourself with the facilities and services available to you.

Passive and dependent students go through orientation because it is on the schedule. They expect that someone will tell them what is important to know. Often that is true. But passive learning makes others responsible for outcomes and does not lead to academic success.

If you are a new student you will probably be going through an orientation program or course. You may receive a college "Survival Kit," which tells you everything you want to know about the school and some things you don't care to know. If, for some reason, you are not going through an orientation program or course, this chapter can serve as your orientation guide.

Whether you use our list or the one given to you by your school, *be active* in acquainting yourself with your school. All of its services were created to help ensure your college success.

REMEMBER: Every office and service at the college exists in one way or another to help you get the college education that you desire. Go find out about these services and take advantage of them!

If you don't get the help or information you need don't go around blaming others. Find some way to succeed!

Your college tries to inform you of every facility and service available to you. Regardless of how hard the orientation leaders try, they are bound to overlook something. This chapter describes the college support services and facilities you should know about. You can use this chapter as your checklist. As you go through whatever form of orientation your college offers, become familiar with all the services and facilities we list that are offered by your college.

If you have completed an orientation program, use this chapter to review your knowledge of campus services. Orientation is a continuous process throughout your matriculation in college. You will need the use of various resources. Make sure you know what they offer and where they are located.

If during your orientation it appears to you that a service or facility isn't going to be mentioned, ask about it. If you still don't find out all you want to know, make sure you search out more information on your own.

Be assertive. Don't stay away from a support service because of rumors or negative advice.

If possible, pay a visit to every service or facility to check it out. For example, most colleges have Learning Skills Centers and Writing Improvement Centers. Often, to find out about what these support services can offer you, you'll need to stop in and have a chat with a staff member. DON'T HESITATE. You'll usually find that staff members of college support services are trying to think up ways to ensure that students make use of their services.

Take a stroll over to the Intramural Sports Center, the Office of Financial Aid, or to any one of the libraries on campus. You may pick up a few ideas about ways in which you want to spend your time on campus. You may learn about financial help you didn't know was available to students such as yourself.

Take the Tour

Most colleges provide guided tours during your orientation program. By all means, take advantage of your orientation tour wherever and whenever it occurs.

During your orientation program, you'll probably be provided with loads of information about the programs, facilities, and opportunities available at your college. If you look around campus, you will probably find free copies of the college newspaper. College newspapers often put out a special "orientation edition" to acquaint new students with the various activities and goings-on on campus.

The checklist of college services and activities we provide below is typical of what you'd often find at a larger school. Whether your college has more or fewer of the places we describe, use our list as a starting point as you acquaint yourself with your campus. The more quickly you become familiar with your campus, the more you will feel at home. Learn why certain offices and facilities exist, even if you don't use them now. At some point it may be to your advantage to know where and why most offices and services exist.

College Orientation Checklist

ORIENTATION DIRECTOR

Go here first. The people who work in this office were hired to help anyone who needs information about starting classes or who has questions about anything to do with being a student

DEAN OF STUDENTS

This is the office to contact if you have any questions or difficulties that are not immediately handled someplace else. The Dean of Students is responsible for seeing that you are well taken care of in school and that any problems you have can be solved. It is likely that if you go to the Dean of Students' office you will be referred to another office. That's okay. The job of this office is to know where to send you and how to find the answers that you want to find.

REGISTRAR

The Registrar's office is responsible for keeping all academic records. This is the office you go to if you are confused about a grade that you have received or if your grade may have recorded incorrectly. If you have taken classes elsewhere, at any time in the past, the Registrar's office can give you information on how to claim credit and obtain documentation so that it will apply to your program. After you graduate, the Registrar's office will provide transcripts if they are requested.

ACTIVITY CENTER OR STUDENT UNION

Here is where the students hang out. You will find cafeterias, art displays, television rooms, reading rooms, possibly a bowling alley, a barber shop, Ping-Pong tables, and pool tables. The student union on every campus is unique, so take time to walk around and familiarize yourself with this building. On the bulletin boards you will find announcements for theater offerings and for the college film offerings. Student groups frequently organize film festivals which show films not available in the reguar theaters in your community.

TRANSPORTATION OFFICE

If you have to commute to school, you may need a permit to park in the campus parking lots. Be sure to find out about carpools and university buses as an alternative to driving your car each day.

FINANCIAL AID OFFICE

Scholarships are only one form of aid or financial support offered to students. There are organizations that provide grants to needy students. A grant is an outright gift, which does not have to be repaid. In some instances, for a person without funds, the college may have a way to reduce tuition fees. Many students can qualify for loans at very low interest rates. These funds are provided by the federal government, and by other sources. If you are a veteran, you probably know about your GI benefits, provided by the federal government, but do you also know that schooling benefits may be provided by your state? The office of financial aid can tell you if you qualify. Another source of funds is through student employment, or "work-study programs." There are many jobs available on campus for students who need income. These jobs don't pay a great deal, but they are on campus and usually have flexible hours to fit with the student's class schedule.

Don't let all the publicity about less money being available for student financial aid hold you back from inquiring. In 1982 the amount of money available dropped by only 4%, but all the publicity about funding reductions reduced applications for aid by as much as 30%.*

Enrollments are down at colleges and universities, so the schools are making special efforts to help students qualify for financial assistance. There are many sources available to students. The office of financial aid has information about assistance available directly from the college itself.

The federal Education Department offers many financial aid programs for students: National Direct Student Loans, Pell Grants, College Work-Study, Supplemental Educational Opportunity Grants,

*Christian Science Monitor, August 31, 1982.

28

PLUS loans, and Guaranteed Student Loans. For a free copy of a booklet describing these sources write to: Consumer Information Center, Department 512K, Pueblo, CO 81009. Ask for "The Student Guide: Five Federal Financial Aid Programs."

Foundations, corporations, and trusts provide over one billion dollars in scholarships and grants each year. The financial aid office will have information about some of these, but there are other sources as well. The National Scholarship Research Service is one of several that for a fee will provide an up-to-date computer print-out of where to apply. Write to: P.O. Box 2516, San Rafael, CA 94912.

If you must work while going to school, don't overlook the possibility of finding a local employer who has a tuition reimbursement program. Many banks, school districts, and corporations reserve funds for employee education and will repay the cost of tuition upon successful completion of courses.

CASHIER'S OFFICE

All monetary matters involving tuition are handled here. *NOTE:* The cashier's office may cash checks for any person with a valid student body I.D. card.

EMPLOYMENT OFFICE

A separate office usually exists to coordinate job offers from local employers with students who are looking for off-campus work. There are many jobs in every community which fit perfectly with being a student. These range from part-time sales work, where you work during hours of your own choosing, to some sort of night work, where you mainly have to sit and watch equipment running.

STUDENT ADVISORS

Your school will have people available to provide academic counseling, meaning they provide information on class schedules, on different courses required for certain majors, your eligibility for certain programs, and such. Their job might be covered by the Dean of Students' office but not necessarily.

ACADEMIC AFFAIRS

This is an important office on every campus. Most likely you will have to go there at some time for assistance with questions or problems having to do with: changing a mistake in your transcript of grades, removing an incomplete in a course, getting permission to take more than the allowed number of course hours, waiving a course requirement, getting into a course already filled, and arranging for special academic programs.

COUNSELING CENTER/CAREER COUNSELING

These offices may be separate or combined. Each has professional counselors available. These counselors are prepared to have private sessions with students who need to talk about personal matters, when certain stresses and problems become more difficult than a person can cope with. The psychologists and/or counselors who work in these centers are specially trained to deal with student problems.

HEALTH SERVICE

Every campus has a medical unit of some kind available for emergency medical care and treatment. It is useful to know where this center is and what services are provided before you need any help from them.

The health service on your campus is probably a resource for information, programs, and services on human sexuality, birth control, prevention of venereal disease, and so on. The health service may also have people trained to deal with alcohol and drug abuse problems.

CAMPUS SECURITY

Find out how to get help from campus security officers in case of an emergency. They are the people to call first when any sort of help from police is needed. *TIP:* Make friends with the security officers. They appreciate it.

STUDENT HOUSING

Your school may provide student housing in its own dormitories. It will also coordinate placement of students in private homes and facilities in the nearby area. Many landlords will register the availability of housing with this office.

STUDY SKILLS CENTER

This center is staffed by specialists in teaching people how to read faster, remember better, pass tests more easily, and, in general, succeed in the academic aspects of school. Improving study skills often is the solution to dealing with "emotional problems."

LIBRARY

Visit the library and take some time to walk through it. You will find that all the stacks are open. You can go almost any place in the library and see what is available. You will notice that in the library there are many, many desks and study areas available. You might consider picking a spot in the library for your regular place to study.

Librarians usually enjoy telling people about all the library services. Take advantage of this good will.

Plan to learn, as soon as possible, about how to use the microfilm equipment. It is not as complicated as it may look to you. Many library materials are stored on microfilm, so it is important to learn what to do if you need to use the equipment.

MUSEUMS AND ARCHIVES

Many colleges and universities have received museums and archives from private donors. Historical collections may be housed in their own buildings somewhere near campus. Find out about these unusual opportunities. The staff will appreciate your interest and you may get much more of an education than you might expect by exploring these places.

LEARNING CENTER

Many schools have established special centers where you can go to learn a specific subject. You check in and tell the person in charge what you want. You will then likely be assigned to a booth with a set of earphones, a television monitor, or a computer terminal. You work at your own speed at the lesson you are there to learn or complete and can stay with it as long as you wish. The person in charge will be glad to explain to you how everything works.

WOMEN'S CENTER

Women returning to school, particularly those with families, often have more difficulties than most men do. To assist women with the unique problems that they must cope with, most schools have established a women's center. This is staffed by very capable and experienced women who are particularly skilled at helping other women cope with the problems they face in being students.

ADULT CENTER

This may be called the Seniors' Center or Gray Panthers' Office. Most schools now have at least one room where older students can get information about any problems or concerns or questions that may come up.

SPORTS CENTER

Be sure to check the sports facility. As a student, you have access at certain times to the gymnasium, the swimming pool, the racquet ball courts, and the tennis courts. Take your time to inquire because having a nice swim between classes some day might be exactly the right thing for you. There will be an exercise room which you can use when available and there may be a track for jogging, basketball courts, and other facilities for exercise.

DAY-CARE CENTER

If you have preschool children, the college may provide day care so you can bring the child with you and for a low fee have the child cared for and fed by professionals while you are in school. This may be for all day or only for several hours.

BOOKSTORE

Take some time to go through the bookstore. Browse around to see where different books are located. Usually the front part of the store contains what is called "trade" books. These are books available to the general public and found in almost all bookstores. At the back of the store you probably will find the textbook section. The books will be arranged on shelves by course numbers within the different departments of the college. The bookstore will probably have ordered and stocked the books you will need for courses that you will be taking. Instructors must place their orders several months before classes start so textbooks are available when you arrive.

NOTE: After registering for your courses, it is wise to purchase your textbooks right away. If you wait until the first class meeting to hear the instructor tell you what to buy, the bookstore might be sold out. Also, if the instructor is using the same textbook again this year, you may find used copies of the book available. Be careful to purchase only the most recent edition of a textbook, however. Using the third edition of a textbook when the instructor has now switched to the fourth edition will not be acceptable.

AROUND CAMPUS

As you travel around campus, you will encounter small groups of students encouraging you to join in their activities. You will find activity groups that are interested in having you become a jogger, hiker, bike rider, chess player, and perhaps player of "new age" video games. You may be invited to join the school choir or band. There are many action groups on campus which will seek your support. Be prepared to have students ask you to sign petitions, to support the development of solar energy, to save whales, to mobilize efforts to fight world hunger, to stop the development of nuclear power plants, to fight the dumping of poisonous waste materials into the earth and water, to free political prisoners, to control the world's population explosion, to control animal population through neuter and spay programs. Whether or not you support any of these activities, the fact is they are a part of campus life today.

During your tour, find out how to qualify for the Dean's honors list and what it would take to qualify for Phi Beta Kappa. Consider setting your goals high. You may be more capable than you realize! Be active in finding out everything you can about your school.

REMEMBER: *The entire school exists to assist you in succeeding in getting the education you want!* Take time now, before you get into your academic program, to get acquainted with your school. You will feel more comfortable more quickly, become more fully absorbed in classes, and enjoy the excitement of learning and discovering new ideas without being confused about what's going on around you.

Action Project: Around Campus

As an aid to getting yourself oriented to your college, list the places on campus that you would like to know more about and write out several questions about each that you would like to have answered:

Name of center or service: _____

Questions: _____

_____

_____

Name of center or service: _____

Questions: _____

_____

_____

Name of center or service: _____

Questions: _____

_____

_____

PART TWO

Doing Well in Classes

Chapter 4

How To Set and Achieve Your Study Goals

Do you know that asking questions is the best way to set study goals?

Do you know that learning is speeded by outlining the tasks necessary to reach your goals?

Do you know that a checklist motivates and rewards you?

Do you know what steps to take if you are in danger of flunking a course?

How to Set Study Goals

Why should I set detailed study goals? You need goals so that you will know where you're going in the process of educating yourself. When you know what you want to achieve, you can set your mind to it, achieve it, and stop worrying about whether or not you'll do well in your courses. Setting goals is one of the strongest ways of motivating yourself to study efficiently and effectively.

Students who don't set specific study goals are usually uncertain about *when* they are going to do *what* they have to do in order to pass their courses. If you can determine what you should study to pass a course and set up a schedule to achieve study goals, you'll be in good shape. Now let's make sure you know how to set study goals and design a schedule to achieve your goals.

How do I figure out what my study goals should be? First, you have to ask, "Who or what can tell me what I have to do to pass the course?" The best sources of information are usually

1. Your instructor.
2. Assigned course materials.
3. Course outlines.
4. Course schedules.
5. Other students.
6. Class discussions.
7. Student manuals and programs.

From these sources you will usually be able to tell what important tasks you have to accomplish in order to achieve your goal of passing a course and becoming a more intelligent person.

What types of tasks are usually required of students who wish to pass courses?

1. Passing tests.
2. Passing quizzes.
3. Writing papers.
4. Participating in class discussions and presentations.
5. Completing projects.

What should I consider when scheduling my study tasks? In addition to knowing the types of tasks that you must accomplish, you should know *how, when,* and *where* they should be accomplished.

What questions should I ask when defining tasks and setting up my study schedule?

When must the tasks be completed?
How much time do I have to complete the tasks?
How much can I reasonably expect to accomplish between now and the time the tasks are due?
How can I divide up my studying so that I don't put everything off until the end?
How much should I do each day if I wish to accomplish my tasks on schedule?

Are there specific requirements for the completion of tasks—format, number of pages, references, and so on?

Where will I be required to demonstrate accomplishment of the tasks?

After answering these questions, you'll be better equipped to design an effective schedule for completing tasks. You will know where you are going, how you will get there, and how to recognize when you've arrived.

Scheduling Tasks to Achieve Your Goals

The process of scheduling is quite simple:

1. Determine your goal.
2. Figure out what study tasks you have to perform to achieve your goal and how much time you'll have in which to complete them.
3. Plan to spend specific study periods completing your study tasks.
4. Use a checklist or graph to record your progress as you complete your tasks.

Here's how to set up a schedule to achieve a goal. We shall use a model in which the student's goal is to pass an exam. Our student decides that the best way to achieve this goal is to use the technique of collecting and answering questions that are likely to be on her next exam. Here are the steps we suggest that she follow in scheduling and completing tasks that will lead to her goal.

Steps in Scheduling

Goal: To receive a passing grade on the next test.

Task 1: Determine when and where the next test will be and what material it will cover.

Task 2: Determine the sources of test questions (textbook chapters, lecture notes, study groups, old tests, student manuals, and so on).

Task 3: Determine how many chapters must be read between now and the test.

Task 4: Plan to read a specific number of chapters each week and to generate questions from them.

Task 5: Plan to spend specific study periods each week generating test questions from course notes, old tests, discussion groups, friends, student manuals, and so on.

Task 6: Plan to spend specific study periods each week making and taking practice tests.

Task 7: Design checklists or graphs to record progress in collecting questions and answers, as well as taking practice tests.

Is all that work really necessary? Isn't there an easier way? At first glance it may appear that it is a lot of work to follow all these steps in reaching study goals. A successful study plan must deal effectively with many learning and remembering difficulties, however. (See the list at the beginning of Chapter 5.) So, yes, there is a lot of work involved in being successful in school. The value of a study schedule with plans for reaching specific study goals is that it is a great timesaver and actually makes learning much easier.

Uses of Recording Progress

Keep Yourself on Schedule

What's the purpose of using a checklist or graph to record my progress in completing tasks? Checklists and graphs are probably the most effective means of keeping yourself consciously aware of taking the actions that will lead to your goal. You define the tasks that you plan to accomplish, determine when you'll have time to complete them, record when each task is completed, and reward yourself for completing the task on schedule. That's not so hard, and it will have a tremendous motivating effect on your performance.

Reduce Anxiety and Forgetfulness

We have found that when students keep checklists or graphs, they have less anxiety about whether or not they're studying frequently enough. They find that after establishing a schedule, they're more likely to study and complete tasks. Graphs and checklists serve as reminders of what must be done and when it must be accomplished.

Record and Reward Your Progress

An important suggestion we have is that when you use a checklist or graph, reward yourself for being at places on time and accomplishing specific tasks. Our goal is to help you establish reasonable goals and accomplish those goals. Using graphs or checklists is the best means by which you will be able to record your progress. Checklists and graphs will remind you of your responsibilities and accomplishments. Checklists and graphs say to you, "This is what you have to do today" or "Congratulations for having accomplished _____."

Few students fall by the wayside when they have clear means of establishing goals and of recording and rewarding their progress, provided that they know how to study. If you reward yourself for completing tasks, you'll find that you are more likely to achieve your goals.

Important Steps in Developing a Checklist

What things should I include in my checklist?

1. Specify each of the tasks that you must accomplish to achieve your overall goal.
2. Arrange the tasks in order of importance and according to when each is most easily accomplished.
3. Indicate next to each task when you expect to achieve it.
4. Record next to each task the actual date it has been completed.
5. Record next to each task the reward you will give yourself for having accomplished this task.
6. Record whether or not you have rewarded yourself for having accomplished the task on time.
7. Record whether or not you have rewarded yourself for having accomplished the overall goal.

What would a checklist look like for the student whose goal is passing her next test? Here is an example of what was worked up with one student who wished to pass her test.

Beverly Bailey
Introductory Psychology

Goal: To receive a passing grade on first psychology test of the semester.
Exam date: September 29, 1984
Today's Date: September 1, 1984
Responsibilities: Read Chapters 1–5 in *Understanding Human Behavior: An Introduction to Psychology* by James V. McConnell.

Beverly decided to reward herself each time she completed one of her tasks on time. She set due dates, then recorded when eack task was completed and whether or not she had received her reward. It

Study Behavior	Due Date	Date Completed	Reward	Yes/No
1. Read Chapter 1, and generate questions, answers, and summary	Sept. 2			
2. Read Chapter 2 (same as 1)	Sept. 5			
3. Read Chapter 3 (same as 1)	Sept. 9			
4. Read Chapter 4 (same as 1)	Sept. 16			
5. Read Chapter 5 (same as 1)	Sept. 23			
6. Generate questions from today's lecture and take practice quiz	Sept. 1			
7. Same as 6	Sept. 3			
8. Same as 6	Sept. 5			
9. Same as 6	Sept. 8			
10. Same as 6	Sept. 10			
11. Same as 6	Sept. 12			
12. Same as 6	Sept. 15			
13. Same as 6	Sept. 17			
14. Same as 6	Sept. 19			
15. Same as 6	Sept. 22			
16. Same as 6	Sept. 24			
17. Same as 6	Sept. 26			
18. Generate questions from old test	Sept. 10			
19. Make up and take practice test for Chapters 1, 2	Sept. 7			
20. Make up and take practice test for Chapters 3, 4	Sept. 17			
21. Make up and take practice test for Chapter 5	Sept. 24			
22. Make up and take practice test from all sources of questions	Sept. 27 28			
23. Meet with study group to make up practice test	arrange			
24. Take exam	Sept. 29			
25. Achieve goal: Pass Exam				

© 1965 United Feature Syndicate, Inc.

was important for her to list her rewards so that there was something to motivate her to complete her tasks on time. Too often in the past, she had found that she put everything off until the last minute and became panic-stricken when she realized how much she had to do. Now, whenever she completed a task on time, she wrote "Yes" on the chart, indicating that she had rewarded herself for doing so.

Beverly listed a series of rewards to choose from whenever she completed a task on time. She was free to choose rewards from outside the list, but we encouraged her to develop a list that would motivate her to keep up with her studies.

Beverly's Reward List

1. Going for a walk
2. Reading magazine
3. Eating snack
4. Taking a nap
5. Playing cards
6. Watching television
7. Playing tennis
8. Calling boyfriend
9. Going on date
10. Ice-cream sundae
11. Riding bike
12. Going to a show

Beverly's list of rewards is likely quite different from one you would develop. Perhaps your list would include a back massage or playing

Space Invaders. Remember, everyone works for rewards that he or she values. We encourage you to reward yourself for studying effectively, just as most people reward themselves for going to work by collecting paychecks.

Isn't it rather time-consuming to make checklists? Couldn't the time be better spent by studying? The checklist took Beverly three minutes to make up. Once it was completed, she knew what she had to do and when she had to complete each task. Afterward, she spent less time worrying about whether or not she was doing the right things and whether she was ahead of or behind schedule. The checklist was an excellent investment in the game of learning to study efficiently and effectively. You may use any type of checklist you wish. This one is simply a model with which our students have had much success.

Benefits of Developing a Checklist

What can you guarantee the checklist will do for Beverly? The checklist of specific things to do is very helpful. If you have everything written out in an organized fashion, it is easy to refer to. You can see what needs to be done more easily. You won't be overwhelmed by the amount of information you need to learn. Also, you are much less likely to be surprised by an important test or paper.

Beverly's Completed Checklist

If Beverly follows the behaviors that she outlined, she will, first, have a good set of questions, answers, and summaries for each chapter. Second, she will not be faced with the problem of having put off reading the chapters until just before the exam. She will study the chapters periodically over a month and will finish them at least a week before the test. Third, she will make up questions and answers immediately following her lectures and will practice quizzing herself to prove that she really comprehends the lectures.

Fourth, Beverly will take a practice test for each chapter before she takes a final practice test. Before the exam she will be well prepared and will have spent less time in final review. This change has a tremendous positive effect on most students' digestive tracts and fingernails. Stomachs and fingers often take a beating when students wait until the last minute to figure out what will be on the next exam.

Fifth, Beverly will find out from her friends what they think will most likely be on the exam. Sixth, she will also obtain a fair idea of what will be on this year's test from looking at a copy of last year's

Study Behavior	Due Date	Date Completed	Reward	Yes/No
1. Read Chapter 1, and generate questions, answers, and summary	Sept. 2	Sept. 2	Hour TV	Yes
2. Read Chapter 2 (same as 1)	Sept. 5	Sept. 5	Hour TV	Yes
3. Read Chapter 3 (same as 1)	Sept. 9	Sept. 9	Read mags.	Yes
4. Read Chapter 4 (same as 1)	Sept. 16	Sept. 16	Sundae	Yes
5. Read Chapter 5 (same as 1)	Sept. 23	Sept. 23	Hour TV	Yes
6. Generate questions from today's lecture and take practice quiz	Sept. 1	Sept. 1	Hour nap	Yes
7. Same as 6 *(late)*	Sept. 3	Sept. 4	None	No
8. Same as 6	Sept. 5	Sept. 5	Cards	Yes
9. Same as 6	Sept. 8	Sept. 8	Rode bike	Yes
10. Same as 6 *(late)*	Sept. 10	Sept. 11	None	No
11. Same as 6	Sept. 12	Sept. 12	Ice cream	Yes
12. Same as 6 *(late)*	Sept. 15	Sept. 16	None	No
13. Same as 6	Sept. 17	Sept. 17	Tennis	Yes
14. Same as 6	Sept. 19	Sept. 19	Walk	Yes
15. Same as 6	Sept. 22	Sept. 22	Cards	Yes
16. Same as 6	Sept. 24	Sept. 24	Call Friend	Yes
17. Same as 6	Sept. 26	Sept. 26	Hour TV	Yes
18. Generate questions from old test	Sept. 10	Sept. 10	Sundae	Yes
19. Make up and take practice test for Chapters 1, 2	Sept. 7	Sept. 7	Show	Yes
20. Make up and take practice test for Chapters 3, 4	Sept. 17	Sept. 17	Show	Yes
21. Make up and take practice test for Chapter 5	Sept. 24	Sept. 24	Show	Yes
22. Make up and take practice test from all sources of questions	Sept. 27 28	Sept. 27, 28	3 hours TV	Yes
23. Meet with study group to make up practice test	arrange	Sept. 27	Nap	Yes
24. Take exam	Sept. 29	Sept. 29	Date	Yes
25. Achieve goal: Pass Exam	Exam Grade	92%	Concert	Yes

exam. Seventh, she will be constantly reminded whether she was ahead of, keeping up with, or behind her study schedule. Eighth, she will reward herself for completing each of the tasks leading to her goal of passing the exam.

Finally, Beverly will increase her motivation to study. In fact, in talking to us about this schedule, she became so enthusiastic that she was going to do the first two chapters immediately to get a head start. We suggested to her, however: "Don't let yourself jump ahead; only allow yourself to study for a certain amount of time. When you've finished, reward yourself, and go on to something else."

The Completed Checklist

It is interesting to compare the proposed checklist that Beverly had made out at the beginning of the month with the same checklist after she had attempted to follow her schedule of tasks and to reward herself for completing the tasks on time. As you will see, she chose most of her rewards from her original list. Periodically she satisfied a whim or spur-of-the-moment desire that she hadn't included on her original list of rewards. It is important to notice that she did not have to spend a lot of money to reward herself. By choosing activities that she enjoyed but seldom found time for when going to school, she was able to encourage and reward her good study behavior while keeping herself out of debt.

Many students ask, "But what can I reward myself with? Everything costs so much." Yet students often complain that they never have time to do things they enjoy—playing cards, watching television, riding their bikes, drinking beer, and going out with their friends to enjoy the "good life." Scheduling rewards for completing tasks encourages students to partake of their favorite activities. They have no reason to feel guilty, as so many students do when they take time away from their studies. The rule of thumb is *when you earn a reward for studying, take it, and never, never cheat yourself.*

Notice that Beverly failed on several occasions to complete her tasks on time. Therefore, she did not reward herself. It was important that she receive the reward only when the task had been completed on time, for procrastination had been a big problem for her in the past. She decided it was important that her chart serve as a means of encouraging her not only to complete her work but also to complete work on time.

For other students, punctuality may not be a problem. It would not be necessary to only reward themselves if their tasks were finished on time. But we usually find that if a person begins skipping tasks or finishing tasks later than planned, he or she tends to return to less effective study techniques, like cramming before exams.

Developing a Graph

Important Steps in Developing a Graph

How can I use a graph to record my progress? A graph is a good means of showing the achievement of tasks, which are counted as you complete them. Beverly, for example, might graph the number of questions and answers she has generated from text chapters, lecture notes, old tests, and so on.

When using a graph to record progress, how do I determine whether or not I've reached my goal? Beverly's goal was to pass her test. She knew that if she predicted and answered questions, she was likely to pass it. She asked herself, "How many questions and answers should I generate from lecture notes, chapters, and other sources to ensure that I comprehend the material and pass the test?"

If she had developed 15 questions for each chapter and 6 for each lecture, she would have had 147 questions and answers at the end of four weeks. She would have distributed her work as follows:

Week	Chapters	Lectures	Total Questions
1	1, 2	1–3	48
2	3	4–6	33
3	4	7–9	33
4	5	10–12	33
			147

In making her graph, Beverly would put the number of tasks she had to accomplish on the vertical line. On the bottom, or horizontal, line she would list the amount of time she had to accomplish her tasks. The graph would look like this:

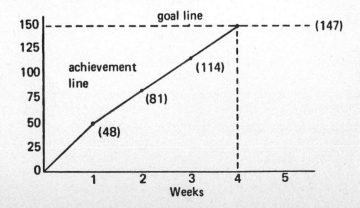

Achievement and Goal Lines

Beverly's goal line is drawn in the figure above. It shows her four-week goal: 147 questions and answers. Had she achieved her goal before four weeks were up, she would have crossed the goal line and continued to develop questions and answers. Most important, she would have known that she had accomplished her goal.

The achievement line is drawn to show the rate at which Beverly had to accomplish her tasks if she wished to reach her goal in four weeks. As she recorded her progress, she would see whether she was ahead of, keeping up with, or behind schedule. If she were behind, she would know it was time to get moving. If she were ahead of or on schedule, she would relax and turn to other activities.

NOTE: The tasks that you must accomplish (number of questions and answers, problems solved, pages read, pages written, and so on) are always listed along the vertical line. The amount of time you have in which to complete the tasks is always written across the bottom line.

Benefits of Graphing

How will the graph help Beverly reach her goal of passing the test?   The graph will tell her how well she is predicting and answering questions that are likely to be on her test. She'll know how much time she has to complete her tasks and how many should be completed each week. She'll know whether she is ahead or behind schedule. The achievement line serves this purpose. She'll be able to record her progress as soon as she completes each task. Finally and most important, though often overlooked, is that the graph will encourage her to reward herself for working to meet her goal.

Rewarding Your Progress

The Importance of Rewards

Why is rewarding myself so important?   Most students try to escape from or avoid adverse situations. Students want to take the pressure off themselves, finish reading the stupid book, get the test over with, and keep from flunking out or doing poorly. In our estimation, this attitude is tragic. Students should enjoy going to school.

We have shown you a series of study skills that will make studying more enjoyable. We would like to increase your enjoyment of studying and doing well in school by encouraging you to reward yourself for accomplishing tasks and achieving goals.

Students often say: "Well, isn't rewarding myself bribery? Why should I reward myself for something I have to do?" The answer is simple: You're more likely to do what's good for you when you encourage yourself to do it. We suggest rewarding yourself with free time, television time, reading magazines, or whatever you enjoy. The rewards need not cost anything. Rewards may simply be opportunities to engage in activities that you enjoy. Go ahead and give yourself periodic rewards for accomplishing tasks.

Guidelines for the Use of Graphs, Checklists, and Rewards

Okay, I'll give the graph and checklist a try. Are there any special rules I should follow in using them? Yes. We suggest, first, that you always *post* your graphs or checklists where they will be highly visible. Your checklists and graphs will serve as constant reminders of what you should be doing and how well you are doing it.

Second, ask yourself what you should really be able to do in the amount of time you have to accomplish your goal. *Schedule* your work, as we suggested earlier, so that all the work for a particular course isn't crammed into a short period of time. Spread your work out! Give yourself time to relax before the test or the date your paper is due.

Third, list the rewards that you will receive for accomplishing your goals. Always reward yourself as you accomplish your goals! Never cheat yourself!

The response from our students throughout the years to using checklists, schedules, and graphs has been exceedingly favorable. Students have enjoyed the benefits of having more predictable study schedules. Needless to say, students have also enjoyed their rewards. Equally important, students have seen improvements in their grades. If you'd like the same results, we encourage you to give these tactics a try.

Where We Are

You now have specific guidelines about two practical ways to organize your time and energies for successful learning. One is to set up a weekly study schedule for yourself. The second is to outline a specific study plan for each test and course assignment. In the chapters ahead you will learn more about why study schedules are so valuable and why asking and answering questions is such an important activity.

Action Project: Setting Study Goals

Directions: Choose one course for which a study checklist would be useful, possibly a course that is more difficult for you than the others. Follow the steps listed on page 41 as you develop your checklist.

At first, use the study goal checklist for only one test coming up in one course. Find out how well this works for you. Then, after trying it out in a limited way and finding that it is helpful, go ahead and work out study goals checklists for all of the courses you are taking.

Use a separate piece of paper for each course and each specific test or assignment within that course. With experience you will discover how nicely using these checklists fits with using a weekly study schedule. You may also discover that it is very rewarding to be able to stop when you have reached your study goal and find that you did not have to take the entire hour reserved!

Action Review: Checklist for Success in Setting and Achieving Study Goals

 Y   N   NI*

1. ___ ___ ___ Do I set specific study goals for each course?
2. ___ ___ ___ Do I set up a schedule to achieve study goals?
3. ___ ___ ___ Do I record my progress at achieving study goals?
4. ___ ___ ___ When I achieve study goals, do I reward myself?

*Y = Yes   N = No   NI = Needs Improvement

Chapter 5

How To Learn More with Less Time and Effort

Do you know how to set up a reasonable and effective plan of study?

Did you know that to reach your educational objectives your study methods must overcome a number of factors that can interfere with learning and remembering?

Do you know how to increase your concentration span?

Are you aware of the ways that visual, auditory, and territorial distractions interfere with study?

When you study, is your approach one that is humanly possible?

Do you reward yourself with breaks as you study?

Learning about Learning and Memory

To succeed in college you must overcome barriers and difficulties that can prevent you from reaching your study goals. Years of research by psychologists have established that the following factors interfere with learning and remembering:

1. People don't learn or retain information well if they are distracted by sights or sounds. In some cases, peoples' inner preoccupations and worries interfere with learning and remembering.
2. People often try to cover too much information too fast.
3. Information may not stick with people. It remains in short-term memory but never gets into long-term memory.
4. People's ability to recall information they have learned drops very sharply immediately following learning. Only a small percentage of information is retained if people do not use or practice relearning it.
5. If people fail to make use of information they have learned, their lack of practice with it will result in loss of memory.
6. Learning of new information will be interfered with by similar information that has been learned before or after the new information.
7. When people have an emotional dislike for material they are learning, they are likely to have difficulties learning it.
8. Should a person lack the desire or intent to learn information or if the information is not viewed as worthwhile, important, or useful, learning and remembering will be hampered.
9. Remembering of information is often difficult because, contrary to their own estimations, people actually fail to learn the information sufficiently well.

Knowledge about the factors that can interfere with learning and remembering helps clarify ways to learn more in less time and with less effort.

Study Regularly

Many students act as though being a successful student is different from being a successful musician with the New York Symphony Orchestra or a tackle with the Pittsburgh Steelers. To be a successful musician or athlete, you need to practice regularly if you want to achieve your learning goals with the greatest amount of pleasure and the least pain. Accept the fact that in college you will have to study almost every day and do more studying than you did in high school.

We suspect that the orchestra conductor would never say to the members of the orchestra, "Our next concert is three weeks away. Let's get together the night before the concert and we'll practice for seven hours." Can you imagine the football coach saying to the team, "Guys, to prepare for next Saturday's game, we'll practice 14 hours on Friday. Until then, have fun and get ready for a real workout!"

Stupid examples? Not really! The conductor and the football coach know that to perform well, you've got to practice frequently for reasonable periods of time. Too much practice too late will make you a physical and psychological wreck.

Like any musician or professional athlete, you need a regular training schedule. You need a study schedule that allows you time to learn everything you need to know at a pace which helps your learning settle in and stick with you for years to come.

Some students really believe they can learn just as much by cramming all of their studying into a few intense study periods before an exam. If you believe this, ask yourself, "Can I bake a cake faster by turning the oven up to 500 degrees? Can I make a garden grow faster by constantly flooding it with water and surrounding it with heat lamps?" No. The same holds true for your learning. That's why your courses are scheduled over several months rather than being crammed into one intensive week of study. Studying for brief periods on a regular basis will lead to better learning than if you try to cram all your studying into a couple of longer periods before an exam.

Most of your courses will require constant preparation and review. As we have noted, some students seem to think that since they may only have a few tests in each course, most of their studying can be done within a week before the test. In most cases, this is a fatal error.

Getting yourself into the habit of keeping up in each course may be difficult for you. This may be especially true if you have a couple of courses that are more demanding than the others. You'll be tempted to spend most of your time on the difficult courses and let the so-called easy courses slide. This is another fatal error.

For years college instructors have been telling students that they need to spend two hours studying outside of class for each hour they spend in class. The truth is that you'll need to spend more time for some classes and less time for other classes.

What it all boils down to is that you need to do the reading and assignments for each class on a regular basis. You want to keep up with each class. You don't want to have that lingering fear that you may be committing academic suicide by letting one class slide until the last minute. Let's look at how you can set up a reasonable schedule.

Set Up Your Schedule

One of your greatest aids will be to use and follow a time schedule. We rate doing this *very highly*. Start by purchasing a monthly calendar with spaces that you can fill in with important dates and obligations. Fill in dates when examinations will take place, when papers and projects are due. Marking these down helps keep you aware of what your studying is leading to. Next, fill in all the times that you plan to go to concerts, shows, family gatherings, meetings; plans for trips or other events; and so on.

After developing a picture of your major commitments for the months ahead, now you are ready to make up a weekly schedule of your classes, study hours, and other obligations. A weekly schedule gives you a clear picture of what you are doing with your time; it helps you spot an extra hour or two during the day that you can use for studying or other responsibilities. This way you can plan more free evenings to do what you want.

Follow these steps for effective scheduling:

1. Establish a well-defined and reasonable schedule, one that you can live with.
2. Budget time to prepare for each class and all examinations.
3. Budget time to take care of all your other personal responsibilities.
4. Study course notes as soon as possible after each class period, rather than waiting until the last few days before the exam.
5. Give difficult subjects preferred times with the fewest possible interruptions and disturbances.
6. Reserve time for leisure activities and make sure that you do not study during these periods!
7. Stick to your schedule and reward yourself for having achieved your study goals in the allotted time.

A good schedule has a motivating effect. Knowing that you have an hour on Thursday morning reserved for studying mentally prepares you to spend that hour doing the studying.

WARNING: Do not allow yourself to study too much. Schedule time for the other things that you want to do and stick to your schedule. Many students become so involved in their studying when they first start using the principles in this book that they keep right on studying through their scheduled breaks. *Don't let yourself do this.* When you reach the scheduled time to stop, go get some exercise or do whatever you want to do. *Learn how to make yourself stop studying!*

Yes, you read us right. For many students, the problem is not studying too little, the problem is that they study so much they are inefficient in their studying habits.

Look at it this way. It is often said that work expands to fill available time. You may have experienced this phenomenon in regard to a project such as cleaning up the house. Let's say that you had in mind cleaning up the house and you had three hours available on Saturday morning. If you have three hours available for cleaning up the house, it will probably take you three hours to get the job done. But let's also say that before you were able to get the job done on Saturday morning, you received a telephone call informing you that a very important person was coming to visit and would be there within 30 minutes. You would probably, in that circumstance, be able to

54

HOUR	Sunday	Monday	Tuesday	Wednesday	Thursday	Friday	Saturday
7-8							
8-9							
9-10	Church	Biolo.	Art	Biolo.	Art	Biolo.	LAUNDRY
10-11		Chem.		Chem.	Review Notes	Chem.	
11-12		Review notes		Review Notes		Review Notes	
12-1							
1-2	Study Biology	Psych.	Psych.	Psych.	Study Art	Biol. lab.	BASKET BALL
2-3	Exam		Psych. Lab.			Biol. Report	
3-4	Study Art	Biol. lab	work-out	Chem. lab		&	
4-5	Exam	Biol. lab	work-out	Chem. lab		Chem. Report	
5-6							
6-7		EVENING STUDY SCHEDULE					
7-8	Study Biology	Study Art	Chem.	Biol.	Psych.	MOVIE	SOCIAL
8-9	Exam	Exam	Biol.	Psych.	Chem.		
9-10			Psych.	Chem.	Biol.		
10-11							
11-12							

clean up the house pretty much to your satisfaction in less than 30 minutes. Part of the approach that we suggest in this book is that you very quickly decide what has to be done, do it, and then stop.

Using a weekly study schedule will show you that you have many more hours during the day than you might have ever realized. You will find copies of the one we have here at the back of the book. Tear them out and use them as you wish.

The partially filled-in weekly schedule appearing above will give you a feel for the types of activities a student can plan for on a weekly basis. Notice how effectively this student can manage her time and her activities by setting up her weekly schedule.

Concentrate while Studying

The key to concentrating effectively is to set a goal for yourself. People who concentrate well focus on achieving a goal they have set. If you decide to study for an hour, ask yourself, "What is my goal for the hour? What will I focus on achieving during the hour? Am I going to read a chapter and answer eight questions about the chapter? Am I going to solve eight calculus problems? Am I going to write an outline for my paper and start the introduction?" Good concentration requires that you set a goal, focus on the goal, and work to achieve the goal.

Eliminate Distractions

Studying at Home

More than likely, your family, roommates, or friends have habits and attitudes that interfere with good studying. These people may have no idea that their behavior bothers you. In contrast, some people will bother you just to get your attention, especially young children.

While you're studying someone turns on the television in the next room. You say, "Please don't turn on the TV, it bothers me." The person says, "I'll keep it low." Someone else walks in and wants to talk or needs to be driven to a friend's house. There is a never-ending barrage of interruptions.

So how do you create a peaceful study atmosphere with all of this craziness going on? If you are like many people, you may try to enforce some rules regarding your study time. We would suggest another approach. Here's why.

"Quiet hours" in dormitories and in people's homes are often a failure. The minute you make rules requiring people to keep noise down or leave you alone, some people seem to go out of their way to demonstrate that the rules can be broken. If you shout, scream, or demand that people keep the noise down, you probably won't get the desired results. Even calm rule enforcement can lead to ruffled feathers and headaches. Rule enforcement requires time which you simply don't need to waste. If you try to enforce rules and people break them, then instead of studying you're sitting there angry, uptight, and furious at what is occurring.

There is a better approach to changing the behavior and attitudes of people around you than making and trying to enforce rules. Whatever the interference is, first ask your friends or family for what you want. Think about what is reasonable and possible. Then ask for it. Be clear, specific, and explain in detail exactly what you would like to have from them. You may be surprised at how understanding and supporting people can be.

Remember, you may be asking the people around you to behave quite differently from what they're used to. Your friends and family's behavior isn't likely to change dramatically overnight. Be patient. Track positives. Notice and appreciate any slight improvement in the direction that you are encouraging. It's up to you to express your appreciation whenever people abide by your wishes. Be sure to express your appreciation and let the people share in your progress.

If you have a friend or family member who is not cooperative, develop a plan for yourself so that you can study and do your course work. Avoid feeling victimized. Instead, come up with a creative plan which will let you continue getting the education you want. Only use strict rule enforcement as a last resort. Remember, your aim is to minimize the amount of time and energy taken away from your real interest, that of studying and learning.

Visual Distractions

Benita is like most students. She has created a comfy nest for herself in her study area. As she closes the door to the den, the wonderful family pictures covering one wall draw her attention. Benita takes several minutes to gaze nostalgically at the photos of herself and Bill at the ocean. The next thing she knows, she's ready to pull out the slides and to heck with her studying. Walking to her desk, she spots a pile of magazines she hasn't had a chance to read. There's the television in the corner. Why not turn it on and catch the last half of the special she wanted to watch? "I can read and watch TV at the same time," she thinks to herself. Everything in the room has a pull for Benita. She feels as though magnetic forces are drawing her to every item in the room.

And that's the trouble. Before she knows it, 20 minutes have slipped away. She glances at the clock and suddenly thinks, "Why have I wasted so much time? Okay. I'll get to work. That's the last time I'll get distracted." That's what she thinks.

As Benita returns to her studies, her mind is distracted from her notes. The family photo on the desk keeps catching her eye. The phone reminds her of several calls she has to make. She starts worrying, "If I don't make those calls tonight, I'll have real problems next week." Before she knows it, she has blown another 15 minutes rehearsing the phone calls that she should be making and daydreaming. Pictures, telephones, magazines, television programs, and such constantly distract her from her studying.

If you study at your desk, keep it cleared off. Don't go berserk and carry the principle too far. We're not suggesting you create a monastic cell with nothing but bare walls and a small light at your desk. What we suggest is that you sit at a desk or in a chair which is comfortable and free of articles that carry memories, free of articles that cry out, "Pick me up, play with me, use me, gaze at me."

Place your desk so that you face a wall that is void of your family history and photos. A blank wall in front of you prevents your eyes from leaving the pages of your notes or text. Place your chair so that you are not looking out a window at the passing scene. Your chair can easily face an area that will not distract you.

To reduce eye strain, your room should be well lit, with the main light source off to one side. A light directly behind or in front of you will be reflected from the glossy pages of your textbooks. A constant glare tires your eyes more quickly than indirect lighting. If you can't shift the lamp, shift your desk. Place the desk so that no portion of the bulb shines directly into your eyes. A strong light source pulls your eyes toward it. The constant strain of trying to avoid looking at the light causes eye fatigue.

Spend a few minutes arranging your study environment. There's no use in feeling uncomfortable. The few minutes you spend will save you hours of distracted study and constant mumbling and grumbling, "I just can't get a thing done. I just can't keep my eyes on the pages. I keep thinking of a thousand other things than studying. And my eyes are killing me!" All of these distractors needn't get in your way if you design your study area to encourage studying and not daydreaming. You need to have the best study area possible.

Auditory Distractions

As we noted, "quiet hours" rarely work as well as the rule makers hope. Distracting sounds still interrupt studying. Doors slam, phones ring, horns honk, and people move around. In fact, the quieter the study area, the more distracting these sounds become.

Steady background sounds can mask distracting noises. Play your radio or stereo softly while you study to create a steady background of "noise" to mask occasional sounds. Experiment with stations or records until you find what works best for you. FM radio stations playing instrumental music are usually best. Talk shows and fast-talking disc jockeys are usually worse for concentration than nothing at all. Some women say that turning on their hair dryers helps them to study. One student reported that he tunes his radio to a place where there is no program. The static keeps him from being distracted.

Don't try to study with the television on. If you want to watch a program, then watch it. But don't try to avoid feeling guilty by having your book open to read during commercials. Studying with your television on is academic suicide. Use television time as a reward. After you have completed a successful study period, say to yourself, "I've earned a reward. I'll watch television."

Territorial Distractions

If you need to escape distractions, GO TO YOUR FAVORITE LIBRARY! Libraries have been designed to help you succeed. People can't yell at you. Your friends can't ask you for attention. Your girlfriend can't bother you with her phone conversation. Your boyfriend won't have "Monday Night Football" blaring. Your roommate can't drag you into a conversation. Only you can prevent yourself from studying in the library. The obvious exception is the nitwit who sits across from you talking to his girlfriend or tapping his pencil. With minor exceptions, most places in a library are good for studying.

When you first go into a library to find a good spot to study, allow yourself a little warm-up time. Whenever you enter a new territory, your senses are drawn to the environment. You automatically scan new surroundings. You check the walls, floor, and ceiling. You look at the lights, decorations, and furnishings. You look at the people, wonder about certain sounds, and spend time adjusting to the feeling of a new chair. Every time you go to a new place to study, you check out the surroundings before you settle down to work. To improve your studying efficiency, pick one spot and always try to study there. Studying in the same spot will shorten your warm-up time and allow you to concentrate better.

If your library is a campus social center, try to find a spot with the least amount of people traffic. Find a remote table or desk where you won't be tempted to watch all the action.

Accept Your Humanness

Concentration Span

Karen is a sophomore English major. During the summer she decided that when she came back to college, she would study three hours every night without interruption. She put a sign on her door:

> Off Limits from 7 to 10 P.M.
> KEEP OUT
> THIS MEANS YOU!

Is she studying more? Yes and no. She can make her body sit at her desk for several hours at a time, but she has a problem that she hardly knows exists. While her eyes look at her book, her mind takes breaks. She sometimes reads several pages and then realizes that she has no idea of what she has read. She has been daydreaming while reading!

59

Does Karen need more willpower? No! She needs to accept the idea that she is a human being. She needs to accept the idea that there are limitations on what the human mind can be expected to do.

The way to make studying easier is to start with what you can do now and build on that. On the average, how long can you study before your mind slips off to something else? Twenty-five minutes? Ten minutes? Most students can concentrate on a textbook 10 to 15 minutes before they start to daydream.

The next time you study, keep a note pad on your desk and notice approximately how long you can read your textbook or notes before you start to daydream. Don't set any particular goals for yourself yet. First, we have to find out what is the typical amount of time you spend reading textbook material before your mind starts to wander. Let's say that you find your average concentration span is about 12 minutes. Now the question is, what would you like it to be—30 minutes, 45 minutes?

Whatever goal you set for yourself, make certain you allow for your humanness. Be realistic. Set a goal that you can reach with reasonable effort and give yourself enough time to reach it. As a rough guideline, you might aim for a time span of 15 minutes by the end of your freshman year, 25 minutes in your sophomore year, 35 minutes in your junior year, and 45 minutes in your senior year. Graduate students should be able to study for about an hour without losing their concentration.

Mandatory Breaks

Once you determine your concentration span, set up your study schedule so that you take a brief break after each study segment and a long break about once an hour. If you do, you will find that you can start and return to your studies much more easily than before.

In fact, you will find the end of a study segment coming so quickly that you will be tempted to continue. *Don't do it.* Keep your agreement with yourself. When you promise to take a quick break after 12 minutes, then do so. *Do not allow yourself to study more than the allotted time.*

A look at the records of most students shows why it is necessary to take these breaks even when you don't want to. With segmented study hours, studying is easier than expected, but after a while the old ways of studying creep back in.

What happens? The critical point comes when you reach the end of a study segment and find yourself so interested in the material that you decide to keep on. If you do, then your mind seems to say, "I can't trust you. You promised me a break after each 14 minutes, but after I fulfilled my part, you kept me working."

When you promise your mind a break after 12 or 14 minutes, *keep your word!* No matter how much you want to keep on, make yourself take a short break. Get up and stretch. Walk out to get a drink of water or a breath of fresh air before starting the next study segment.

Mix Study Subjects

Mark is carrying a full load in school: English, biology, chemistry, psychology, Spanish, and physical education. He studies each day at school and three evenings a week. But when he tries to recall what he has covered in an evening, he has trouble doing so.

Is Mark a slow learner? Probably not. His memory problem is caused by his study schedule. His evening study schedule looks like this:

Hour	Sunday	Monday	Tuesday	Wednesday	Thursday	Friday	Saturday
7–8		Biology	Chemistry	Spanish			
8–9		Biology	Chemistry	Spanish			
9–10		Biology	Chemistry	Spanish			

Mark's memory problem exists because he spends about three hours on one subject. When a person learns one set of facts and then goes on to learn similar facts or material, the second set will interfere with memory of the first and the first will interfere with memory of the second. The more similar material a person tries to learn at one time, the worse his or her recall will be.

How can you avoid this problem when you have lots of material to study? The best way is to mix your study hours with dissimilar material. *Do not devote all of one evening to one subject.* Switch subjects every hour or so. Always try to make your new subject as different as possible from the subject you have just finished. That way your mind can be assimilating one topic while you are reading about another. Mark did much better when he revised his schedule as follows:

Hour	Sunday	Monday	Tuesday	Wednesday	Thursday	Friday	Saturday
7–8			Chemistry	Biology	Biology		
8–9			Spanish	Spanish	Chemistry		
9–10			Biology	Chemistry	Spanish		

Although Mark's new schedule shows that he is mixing dissimilar subjects, he could apply another principle of learning. Research shows that material you memorize is retained better if immediately followed by sleep. Insightful learning can occur at any time and is not vulnerable to what follows immediately. This difference means that subjects like Spanish and chemistry tend to be remembered better if studied immediately before bedtime.

What's Next?

In Chapter 6, we'll continue our focus on time management as we discuss how to set and achieve your study goals. We'll then move on to the keys to successful learning, studying, and test preparation in the following few chapters.

Action Project: Learning about Learning and Memory

1.___ ___ ___ Read the sections on memory and forgetting in several different introductory psychology textbooks.
2.___ ___ ___ Make a list of all the principles and factors that help or hinder learning and memory.
3.___ ___ ___ Look through *Student Success* to see how much the book is organized to use the knowledge of these facts and principles.
4.___ ___ ___ List several techniques you could use on a regular basis to improve your memory.
5.___ ___ ___ Get together with some other students who are motivated to do well in college and talk about what you have learned from this information about learning and memory.

Action Project: Setting Up a Schedule

Directions: Beginning on page 177 you will find schedules that can be removed from your book. Tear out the first schedule and use the suggestions in Chapter 5 to create a weekly schedule. List below all the activities you'll want to be sure to include on your weekly schedule:

1. _____
2. _____
3. _____
4. _____
5. _____
6. _____
7. _____
8. _____
9. _____
10. _____

Post your schedule in a place where you will constantly be able to see it. As you complete the activities during the week, cross off each square that represents an activity you complete.

By keeping track of the activities you complete, you are likely to find that you are motivated to stay on schedule. Notice that we are not trying to encourage you to schedule your entire life. Just schedule the activities which you have to complete for your academic and personal satisfaction. Make sure you leave time for just doing what you please and for all of those spontaneous activities that make life so rewarding. At the end of the week, review your schedule to determine the percentage of activities you have completed. If you feel you have done very well in keeping to your schedule, give yourself a little reward.

Action Review: Checklist for Learning More with Less Effort

	Y	N	NI*	
1.	__	__	__	Have I outlined a weekly study schedule for myself?
2.	__	__	__	Do I write out and follow daily time schedules?
3.	__	__	__	Have I asked people to be considerate of my need to study?
4.	__	__	__	Is my study free of distractions?
5.	__	__	__	Do I mask distracting sounds with soft music or some other steady background noise?
6.	__	__	__	Have I arranged good lighting?
7.	__	__	__	Do I study in the same place each time?
8.	__	__	__	Do I avoid studying one subject too long?
9.	__	__	__	Have I determined my concentration span and set up study segments geared to my present ability?
10.	__	__	__	Do I take short breaks after study segments and a long break each hour?

*Y = Yes   N = No   NI = Needs Improvement

Chapter 6

Becoming More Successful in Your Classes

Do you know what it means to be an active learner?

Have you discovered the value of asking good questions?

Do you know that your intelligence is revealed more in the questions you ask than in the answers you give?

Do you know that the "SQ4R" method is the most widely used and effective way to study?

Do you know that most lectures can be viewed as a series of questions and answers?

Do you know how to use lecture notes for exam preparation?

Do you know that your studying time can be reduced by concentrating on developing test questions?

Do you always look for possible test questions and answers as you read?

Do you always study as though you were practicing to take a test?

What does being "intelligent" mean to you? Would you say that intelligent students have good vocabularies, are very knowledgeable, and solve problems easily? Are intelligent students able to answer their instructors' questions and get high scores on tests? If one of your goals in life is to be an "intelligent" person, then it's important for you to decide just what it is that you should know and be able to do!

Most college students believe they are intelligent people. A favorite pastime of many students and instructors is to discuss: "What is intelligence? Is it inborn? Can it be increased? Is an intelligent person creative? A wise decision maker? An independent thinker? Is there more than one kind of intelligence? If so, what different kinds are there?"

Our bias is to look for behaviors that are associated with intelligence. Most psychologists agree that an intelligent person is an efficient learner. He or she learns and remembers more than other people. But what behavior leads to this? *Asking and answering questions.* An intelligent person asks important questions and searches for the answers.

Take vocabulary, for example. Most clinical psychologists believe that vocabulary is the best single indicator of intelligence. How does a person acquire a good vocabulary? By wondering "What does that word mean?" and then finding the answer.

One good means of finding answers to vocabulary questions is to obtain a good, inexpensive dictionary and use it. Equally useful is to ask what people mean when they use certain terms. Search for the best words to describe something. Searching for information and answers to questions will help make you successful in school.

Asking Questions: Key to Efficient Learning and Success in Classes

If you lean back in your chair and analyze what you must do to be a successful student, it will be clear to you that you must ask and answer good questions. You must do so when writing papers, reading your texts and notes, talking in discussion groups, attending classes, and taking tests.

Think of your textbook. It consists of answers to a lot of questions. Your instructors spend much of their time developing questions to ask you in class and on tests. Think of the notes you take. Are they anything more than answers to questions? Your instructors have carefully analyzed important books, lectures, films, and other resources to generate a body of information which they present to you in class. The final task for you is to answer important questions about this information.

Let's look at simple and highly effective learning techniques developed at the University of Michigan. Students using these techniques report that once they learn to ask and answer intelligent questions, they become more successful in school. They save hundreds of hours in studying and preparing for courses. As a result, they are able to spend more time going to movies, watching television, playing sports, being with friends, taking weekend trips, attending concerts, and leading the "good life."

If these things interest you, then let's spend a little more time discussing how you can learn the correct techniques. One thing we promise is that you will achieve your academic goals with a great deal more pleasure and far less pain than you have known in the past. We must sound one word of caution: This goal may require you to change many of your old habits. Such changes are sometimes difficult or painful.

Why? Well, when you are used to a standard set of procedures to accomplish your goals, you often become comfortable with them and resist change. Even if you try the new study techniques, you'll have a tendency to go back to your old study behaviors. These old behaviors will help you to accomplish your goals to a degree, but with the same pain and tremendous number of hours that you have spent in the past. Once you become accustomed to the new study techniques, a lot of your old self-defeating behavior and attitudes related to studying and becoming educated will fade away. You will begin to get some good feedback from professors, friends, and yourself indicating that the new methods save time. You will achieve your goals and have time to do things you never had time for in the past. Here we go!

Principle 1: Study To Pass Tests

Whenever you are reading out of curiosity, allow your mind to go in any direction it wishes. But when you study, *study as if you were practicing to take a test.* Practice answering questions! If you don't, you are wasting your time! Remember, it's your time, so why waste it?

Doesn't studying as if you were practicing to take a test go against the idea of simply learning for the sake of learning? It might if you are attempting to learn the material by rote and experience it as meaningless. When you focus your reading and studying by looking for answers to questions, you make the material meaningful and learn significantly more. Whether or not you are going to take a test on the material you are reading is secondary. Your main aim is to develop the habit of getting the most out of your reading. To get the most out of your reading you need to focus on looking for answers to questions.

66

Principle 2: Ask Intelligent Questions

What is an intelligent question? First, it is one that you would like answered. Second, it is framed so that in seeking the answer you will learn new and useful things. Third, it might be close to one your instructor asks on a test. Fourth, it can be a way to demonstrate what you already know.

How do you learn to ask intelligent questions? This question itself is a good one. Practice is the answer. Practicing is a useful personal habit to acquire. At first it takes some work, but later questions will arise out of habit.

What will good questions help you do? Are you and your instructor interested in the same thing? You'll only know by asking questions. You may wish to study information that is of no interest to your instructor. That's fine. But regardless of your own interests, you want to make sure you do well in your course by knowing the information your instructor defines as important.

If you ask good questions, you'll be able to focus on the important points of your lectures and readings. Good questions help you discriminate what your lecturers and the authors of your texts believe you should remember.

A major function of your questioning process should be to prepare you for exams. By practicing answering the questions you develop, you'll find out just how ready you really are to "ace" your exam. After all, have you ever taken an exam that wasn't composed of questions your instructor wanted you to answer? That's why we cannot overemphasize the value of proving your brilliance by answering your questions!

Another point not to be overlooked is that you will please your instructors no end if you ask and answer good questions in class. The hundreds of hours you'll save in preparing to do well in your classes and on exams is clearly one of the hidden bonuses of the question-and-answer regime we recommend.

What does a good question look like? It usually starts with a phrase like:

Give several examples of _____
Which of these is an example of _____
Describe the function of _____
What is significant about _____
List the important _____
Compare and contrast _____
Interpret the following _____
What is the structure of _____

Identify the following _____

Why does _____

A complete good question might look like:

Why do both your hunger "pangs" and your stomach contractions tend to decrease after lunchtime even if you didn't eat anything?

How would you go about testing your auditory threshold?

Compare the major psychological differences between chimpanzees and humans.

Give several examples of imperialism in South Africa during the early 1900s.

What functions are associated with the two hemispheres of the brain?

Generate Intelligent Questions

How can I determine what the important questions are? Pretend that you are the instructor and generate questions from your texts, lecture notes, and old exams. Think of questions before you go to class and then listen to find out whether or not other students ask the same questions and whether or not the instructor supplies answers to those questions.

Write out questions for a lecture or an assignment. Then ask your instructor whether he or she thinks these questions are important and what other questions you should attempt to answer.

Do not be afraid to ask your instructor what he or she thinks are the important questions! Most instructors are happy to tell you what they think is important. Give them a chance, and they'll take a mile!

Ask your professor what goals he has for the students in his class. If you want a clear answer, you must learn to ask questions that help him clarify for himself the questions he would like the class members to answer. You might ask:

"What should we be able to do and what important questions should we be able to answer after having completed this chapter (unit, training, program)?"

"What important questions do you think we should be looking at in this unit (chapter, assignment)?"

"Can you suggest particular articles or books that highlight the issues we will be discussing in this unit?"

"What important things should we be looking for in this particular reading (film, case study)?"

Such questions should be asked in as positive a manner as possible. Students have a tendency to put instructors on the defensive. It is your job to ask an instructor in what direction the course is headed and to reward him for telling you. A comment like "Thanks, that really clarifies things for me" is something an instructor appreciates.

Now that I know what intelligent questions are, what is the best way to get into the habit of developing questions and answers? We prefer to start by showing you how you can get a lot more out of your reading by turning it into a question-answering process. We'll then get into note taking, test taking, and a variety of other important study skills, but reading is the most important, so that's where we'll begin!

Reading = Question Answering

READ TO FIND QUESTIONS AND ANSWERS

Studying is not the same as reading your Sunday newspaper. Reading your textbook is not the same as casually reading a novel or light fiction. Most textbooks are not written to entertain you. You can't get away with reading only the parts of texts that interest you. When it comes to studying, you must use reading techniques that motivate you to mentally and emotionally reach out and grasp important information.

Studying can be fun, but sometimes studying is very hard work, as hard as any physical labor. Passively reading your textbooks and lecture notes over and over again is no fun and is an inefficient way to learn course material. So how do you make reading pay off? How do you read to comprehend all the important information you'll need to know?

Remember one tip! Your reading of textbooks and notes must be geared to help you prepare for doing well on tests, meeting course requirements, and developing an understanding of what you're studying.

> SUCCESSFUL STUDENTS VIEW TEXTS AND NOTES AS SOURCES OF QUESTIONS AND ANSWERS THAT ARE LIKELY TO APPEAR ON THEIR EXAMS. Keep in mind, *if you are not reading and studying textbooks and notes as if you are preparing to take a test, you are wasting your time!*

Increasing Your Reading Speed and Comprehension of Textbooks

One of the fastest ways to spend less time reading assignments is to learn how to figure out the important questions and answers as quickly as possible. First, you should know that a large percentage (perhaps as many as 80%) of the words you read are unimportant.

Most words simply link ideas. The ideas are the answers to the questions you wish to answer.

Second, you already know much of what you have to comprehend. As you survey and read, what you want are the answers to questions that you generate or find in the chapter. Dozens of studies with college students show that the following steps will improve your reading speed, comprehension, concentration, and memory.

Reading Chapters in Textbooks

Survey—Question—Read—Recite—
Write—Review = The SQ4R Method

Remember, improved comprehension is the ability to answer more questions from reading assignments. This approach to reading is considered by many experts on study skills and reading improvement to be the most efficient and effective means for getting the most out of reading material in the least amount of time. The primary concern of students using this method will be to *ask* and *answer* intelligent questions as they read.

What you should do is described in the following sections.

Survey and Question

The goal of surveying is to determine what important questions are answered in the textbook chapter. First, go to the beginning and end of the chapter to see whether or not there are chapter objectives, a list of questions, or a chapter summary. If so, read them right away! This is where you will find the important points that authors wish to stress and the questions students should be able to answer after completing the chapter.

If you can answer the questions and already know what is in the summary or chapter objectives, you probably won't have to read the chapter. But don't decide yet. If there is a set of questions, a list of objectives, or a chapter summary, you're ahead of the game; if not, you soon will be.

How do you survey? *The process of surveying involves quickly skimming the chapter to determine what important questions it answers.* Look for titles, subtitles, illustrations, pictures, charts, lead sentences in paragraphs, and questions that will give you a basic idea of what the chapter is about.

While surveying, it is easy to turn titles, subtitles, and lead sentences into questions. For instance, "Communist Techniques of Brainwashing" is a paragraph heading in *Understanding Human Behavior,* a textbook written by James McConnell. You simply turn it into "What were the techniques of brainwashing used by the Communists?"

By generating questions as you survey, you keep yourself alert to the important points in the chapter. Reading becomes an active, goal-oriented process. As you survey, you should formulate questions that, when answered, will give you a good summary of the chapter. *The result of your survey will be a list of questions.*

To prove your brilliance, you may wish to attempt to answer the questions you have generated in your survey before reading. This attempt serves to tell you how much you already know before spending an exorbitant amount of time reading. Many students are amazed at their ability to answer a large percentage of the questions they have formulated in their survey.

Another helpful technique is to quickly summarize what you already know about the chapter. By talking to yourself about the chapter, you help yourself focus on the important questions you should be able to answer after having read it.

Read To Answer Questions

It is now time to read: Read as quickly as you can. Read to find the answers to questions you have generated while surveying the chapter and to find new questions and answers that you haven't predicted while surveying.

REMEMBER: In many instances, your questions and answers will be found in titles, subtitles, or lead sentences. Occasionally, you may have to read beyond this information for more important details. But not with the regularity that caused you to waste a lot of time in the past when you were looking for unimportant details.

When reading to answer questions, you first predict important questions before spending a lot of time reading. You then read selectively. You read rapidly to find answers to questions. When you come to the answer to a question that you hadn't predicted, you simply slow down, formulate the question, and make sure you know the answer. When you come to material you already know, keep on going to find out what you don't know.

Recite and Write Answers and Summaries

Now that you have (1) read to answer the questions from your survey and (2) developed new questions and answers that you hadn't predicted, it is important for you to go one step farther.

Recite and write answers to the questions you developed while surveying and reading. After you have recited and written the answers to your questions, take a minute to summarize the chapter aloud. By talking to yourself about the answers to your questions and relating them to one another in a summary, you'll help improve your understanding of how all the concepts fit together. These procedures are an excellent means of proving to yourself that you have asked and answered the important questions from each chapter.

Don't hesitate to talk to yourself (even if people think you're a little crazy) about the answers to your questions. Often students rush on to a new chapter before thoroughly proving to themselves that they are familiar with the contents of the chapter they just read. They say to themselves, "I read it. I know what it's about." DON'T MAKE THAT MISTAKE! Prove to yourself by answering questions and verbally summarizing that you really do comprehend the chapter.

Review

If you have followed the steps so far, you are in excellent shape to review the chapter at any time. You will have a set of questions and answers representing the contents of the chapter. When preparing for your exam, quiz yourself on these questions until you feel comfortable that you could give accurate answers to them if they were to appear on your exam.

We also suggest summarizing to yourself, orally or in writing, the contents of the chapter and comparing your summary with the author's summary at the end of the chapter.

Taken together, these activities will really give you the feeling that you've mastered the material. When you know you can answer questions correctly and make accurate summaries, you will be more confident that you have mastered the chapter.

The Result

You have now

1. Surveyed the chapter.
2. Generated questions.
3. Read selectively to answer the questions in greater detail.
4. Found questions and answers that you hadn't predicted.
5. Recited and written answers to questions.
6. Summarized the chapter aloud.
7. Reviewed the chapter by practicing answering questions and summarizing the chapter.

You now have a good understanding of the chapter.

Take This Book, for Example

For an example of how to use SQ4R, look at how this book is organized. "About this Book" gave you an outline of the contents. Next, in "How To Use This Book," we urged you to skim rapidly through the book to answer questions about it. Now you are reading the book in greater detail and talking over the new things you are learning with your orientation class or your study partners.

At the end of most chapters you find an "Action Review." The review questions help you specifically determine whether or not you are putting into practice what you are learning.

We wrote this book in a way which helps you put into practice what we know works for students!

Why should I believe that this approach works?   Evidence collected at the University of Michigan Reading and Learning Skills Center and other learning centers has shown that most good students use these techniques. When poor students learn SQ4R, they raise their grades, reduce study time significantly, increase reading speed, and improve comprehension of textbooks.

Advantages of SQ4R

With SQ4R you spend less time memorizing facts that you will soon forget. You don't waste time reading and looking for things you already know. Your preparation for tests is a continual process. By the time you take the test, you will find that you have answered most of the questions. You focus on grasping the key concepts. Details are then much easier to remember. You don't waste time looking for details that are unimportant to you or your instructor. You learn to take an expert's point of view and to think things out for yourself. You learn to sit down and generate answers that you didn't think you knew. You then search for additional information, which makes polished answers out of incomplete ones. You learn to organize and structure your studying. You state your goals as questions, seek answers, achieve your goals, and move on.

Difficulties of SQ4R

It is difficult to change old study habits. You may be accustomed to reading every word, always afraid that you're going to miss something. A new technique such as the SQ4R method may appear reckless because you learn so fast. It takes more energy to ask questions and generate summaries than it does to let your eyes passively read printed pages. It is easier just to open a book and start reading. With SQ4R, you study a little bit frequently instead of waiting until the end of the course and cramming.

How can you reconcile advantages and disadvantages? There are advantages and disadvantages to *everything*! This is true for both successful and unsuccessful students. If there were no disadvantages, if it were easy, then everyone would be more successful. There are costs, but once you are into SQ4R, the gains are worthwhile.

Imagine yourself agreeing to run in a 10-kilometer race several months from now. You will be running with friends, and it is important for all of you to do well. To be at your best, would you loaf around until the last few days and then prepare by running day and night until the time of the race? No. You'd start now with a weekly schedule of jogging and running. A little bit of practice on a regular basis prepares you the best. The same approach is true for effective study and remembering.

Try the study techniques and look for results like the following:

The quality of your questions and answers will improve with practice.

The amount of time it takes you to generate questions and summaries will decrease.

The amount of time it takes to verify and improve your answers will decrease with practice.

You will be able to cover large amounts of material in far less time.

You will find that you are producing the same questions as your instructors, textbooks, and friends.

With practice, you will find that the summaries you generate come closer to those of the author.

These techniques are based on several well-established learning principles. First, when you learn material under conditions that are similar to those under which you will be tested, there is a greater likelihood that you will remember it. People learn meaningful material faster than they memorize unrelated or nonsensical information. Learning new material is easier when you associate it with familiar material.

The SQ4R method sounds helpful, but could I start by just using parts of the technique or using the whole technique on small sections of my work? Our students report best results when they begin practicing the entire technique at once. But some people will adjust best to the SQ4R strategy by practicing on a small section of work in one course to see immediate results. They gradually increase the use of this method as they become more comfortable with it.

Predicting Exam Questions

How do I go about predicting exam questions from sources other than my text? Once you accept the value of always studying as if you were practicing to take a test, you'll be on the right track. It is important to gear your study behavior to collecting questions and answers that you expect to find on your exams. By using the reading techniques that we have suggested, you will have a good start. Your reading will always be geared to asking and answering important questions.

In addition to this style of reading, there are several other techniques that will help you collect a good set of exam questions. Note taking, asking friends and instructors, collecting old exams, holding discussion groups, and using textbook and student manual questions are several that we suggest. Let's start with note taking in class.

Sources of Exam Questions

Be an Active Learner

ATTEND CLASS

Attending class is such an obviously useful thing to do that we're almost embarrassed to have to mention it. Yet, in a research study reported by H. C. Lindgren,* it was found that there is an important relationship between attending class and grades received. A comparison of grade point averages and class attendance showed these percentages:

Class Attendance	% of Students with B Average or Higher	% of Students with C− Average or Lower
Always or almost always present	85	48
Sometimes absent	8	7
Often absent	7	45

The percentages in the table suggest that attending class always or almost always helps maximize your chances of success. For the student who is often absent, the percentages indicate that the student will probably receive low grades.

THE FIRST LECTURE

Successful students are active in determining the requirements for each course. They use their study time to engage in behavior most likely to help them achieve course success. During the first lecture, find out answers to these key questions:

Which chapters in the textbook will be covered?
When will the exams be given?

*Henry Clay Lindgren, *The Psychology of College Success* (New York: Wiley, 1969), p. 50.

What material will each exam cover?

What type of questions will be on the exams—essay, multiple-choice?

What other work will be required?

When will the work be due?

How will the work be evaluated?

How will grading in the course be determined?

Does the instructor have an outline of the most important terms and concepts to be covered?

Should textbook chapters be read before lectures?

What does the instructor hope each student will understand by the end of the course?

These questions are a starting point. Others will occur to you as you go along.

A WORD OF CAUTION: Don't make instructors feel that they are being cross-examined. Be assertive, but *tactful*. If an instructor is not prepared to answer all these questions, back off. Try to find out when the information may be available. In general, you will find that instructors enjoy answering questions about what they believe is most valuable in their courses. A few instructors may be poorly prepared, however, and could become defensive if pressed too hard.

Some instructors will have the answers to most of these questions on written handouts. If you don't receive a handout, be sure to write everything down in your notebook.

TAKE LECTURE NOTES

By writing down what the instructor says in lectures, you are helping yourself become an active listener. You are also being realistic about the nature of human memory. Human beings quickly forget most of what they hear, no matter how much they would like to be able to remember.

Several days after hearing a lecture, most students can at best recall only about 10% of what was said. So, unless you tape-record the lectures or alternate note taking with a friend, you need to take notes at every lecture.

Some students don't take notes. They may be trying to experiment to see whether or not they can get by without note taking. These students may have reasons for wanting everyone to know that they are not involved in the course. They may be trying to impress you with how smart they are. At any rate, if you ask a student who doesn't take notes to fill you in on something the instructor said last week, you will quickly learn for yourself how important note taking is for accurate remembering.

USE LECTURE NOTES AS A SOURCE OF
EXAM QUESTIONS AND ANSWERS

You should accustom yourself to thinking of your instructor's lectures as sessions which provide answers to important questions. You should actively use your notes to quiz yourself on important questions that are likely to appear on your instructor's exams.

REMEMBER: Use your notes to learn more and do better on your exams. If you remember the formula: NOTES = EXAM QUESTIONS AND ANSWERS you'll learn a lot, do well on your exams, and live happily ever after!

Lecture Notes

Think of your lectures as textbook chapters. Just like a chapter, each lecture usually has a main theme and makes several important points. If you listen for the main points of each lecture, they will be easier to hear.

During lectures, most instructors answer several questions rather thoroughly. If your instructor only alludes to an answer, you'll have to go to outside sources to get the information you need.

Your job during the lecture is to record the most important information given. Don't restrict your note taking to only those statements made by the instructor. Be alert to classroom discussions in which students are asked questions by the instructor. After the lecture, use study time to develop questions that are answered by information in your notes.

TIPS ON TAKING NOTES

Keep a notebook for each course. Write your name, address, and phone number in each notebook. Use large pages for taking notes. Put the notes from each class on separate pages. Put the date on each day's class notes.

Use an outline form whenever possible. The most commonly used outline form is this:

    I. (Roman numerals for major topics)
       A. (Capital letters for major subgroups)
          1. (Numbers for supporting examples, people, points)
          2.
       B.
          1.
             a. (small letters for supporting details)
             b.
             c.
          2.
          3.

We encourage you to take lecture notes in an outline form. This habit will help you focus on listening for and recording main points that you can turn into questions and answers. We suggest the outline form because it helps create an orderliness to information that might otherwise appear confusing. Our chief concern is that you record all the information you need to develop good questions and answers. The following hints will help ensure that you listen for and record the main points of every lecture.

STEPS FOR TAKING NOTES

1. During each lecture, take notes on the right-hand side of the paper. Leave a two-inch margin on the left. You'll use this margin later as space in which to write your questions.
2. Write down the major ideas and statements in the lecture. Don't try to write down every word, just key phrases and ideas. Underline points that your instructor emphasizes.
3. After the lecture, fill in missing ideas and key words and phrases. Underline headings that are of major significance. You may also wish to compare your notes with a friend's to see what you may have missed.
4. After each lecture, take several minutes to turn your notes into questions. The main theme and subtopics can be turned into questions. Each lecture will usually supply you with three to seven good exam questions. The questions should be written in the left-hand margin.
5. At least once a week review the questions you have asked. Pretend that you are taking a test. Give yourself an oral quiz, or, even better, practice by taking a written quiz. Then compare your answers with those given in your notes or textbook.

REMEMBER: This procedure will help make something meaningful out of lectures that often leave you in a quandary. Your purpose is to go to lectures looking for questions and their answers. If you come out of each lecture with several questions and answers, you'll be pleased. They're likely to be on your next test!

Your notes may not look as neat as those below. We don't expect you to carry a typewriter to class. If your notes are neat and as close to outlined as possible, you'll have a much better chance of turning them into a good set of questions. These notes were taken at an introductory psychology lecture. The topic was operant conditioning.

Intro Psych—Oct. 26th
I. Topic: Operant Conditioning

Questions

    A. B. F. Skinner conducted pioneering research
      1. worked with rats and pigeons
      2. designed special cages—"Skinner boxes"

What is an important belief of B. F. Skinner?

3. believes "Behavior is determined by its consequences"

What is another term for operant conditioning?

Why do psychologists use the term "reinforcement" instead of "reward"?

B. Basis for operant conditioning (also called instrumental learning)
1. a voluntary behavior is followed by a reinforcer—not called a reward because some rewards do not act as reinforcers
2. reinforcement increases the probability that a behavior will be repeated
3. reinforcement variables:
   a. amount
   b. schedule
      1. 100%—continuous
      2. fixed-ratio and fixed-interval
      3. variable-ratio and variable-interval

Will punishment usually eliminate behavior?

4. punishment can temporarily suppress behavior but seldom eliminates it
5. negative reinforcement—behavior increases when unpleasant stimulus removed
6. extinction of behavior
   a. from withdrawal of reinforcer
   b. after time lapse reappearance called spontaneous recovery

What is spontaneous recovery?

How is a behavior modification program conducted?

C. Application of principles
1. Behavior modification program
   a. terminal response or goal stated—must be observable and measurable
   b. current level of desired behavior observed—called baseline
   c. any baseline behavior directed toward the terminal goal is reinforced; all other behaviors ignored
   d. each small step is reinforced—is called:

What terms are used to describe the method of reinforcing any small step in the right direction?

      1. shaping
      2. method of successive approximations
      3. tracking positives
2. Uses with humans—contingency management
   a. programs for brain-damaged children
   b. improve academic performance
   c. programs for psychiatric patients
   d. improve performance in business

Old Exams

Students often feel guilty when they admit to having looked over past exams. They feel that they have been cheating. Our answer to this is, bunk! Looking at old exams tells you what an instructor thinks is important information for which students should be responsible.

Looking at old exams doesn't guarantee that you'll know exactly what your exam questions will be. Instructors change their lectures, textbooks, films, guest speakers, and even their opinions once in a while. Consequently, exams change from semester to semester.

Nevertheless, by looking at old exams you may answer several important questions:

1. Does the instructor have some favorite questions that he or she asks every year?
2. Do test questions appear to be taken from material similar to that which you are studying?
3. Do test questions come primarily from lecture notes or from a variety of sources?
4. What types of questions does the instructor prefer: multiple-choice, short-answer, true-false, essay?
5. On which content areas does the instructor place the most emphasis?

These questions should help you see the value of reading and taking notes in the question-answer format. There is no guarantee that the instructor will take most of the questions from the same source that he or she used in years past. Yet it is surprising how similar questions are from year to year regardless of the textbooks used by instructors. They often choose new textbooks that give better answers to the same questions they have been asking for many years. Equally important, few instructors make drastic changes in their course notes from semester to semester. They usually only update notes. The questions you generate from course notes, textbooks, and other sources, combined with old exam questions, will be invaluable in your exam preparation.

Textbooks

Always read the questions that precede or follow the chapter. Such questions are included by authors because they believe that students should be able to answer the questions after having read the chapter.

Many instructors take their test questions directly from those in the textbook. Surprisingly, many students never look at textbook questions. They seem to feel that no instructor could be so stupid as to use questions similar to those found in the chapter.

Authors and instructors usually try to help students, not trick them! If you are not in the habit of answering chapter questions, we recommend you use them as the starting point in your effort to organize a good set of questions and answers.

Student Manuals

Always use the student manuals that accompany many textbooks as sources of exam questions. Student manuals are designed to inform you of the study behaviors that will be helpful to students using the textbook. Manuals often contain true-false, multiple-choice, fill-in, and short essay questions. Even if your exam is likely to be made up of questions that differ in style from questions found in the student manual, the manual questions are still valuable.

You only have to relate the manual questions to the questions likely to be found on your next exam. Don't avoid student manuals that are in a programmed format. Student manuals are designed to save you time. Whatever the format of the student manual, use the manual as a source of exam questions. The time you save by using a student manual can be used for other important activities, like watching television or taking a nap.

NOTE: *The publisher of your textbook may have a student manual available even if the instructor did not require its use.* Check this out—especially for introductory textbooks. If a student manual exists, you can purchase it through the bookstore or directly from the publisher. Sales figures from textbook publishers show that 7 out of 10 students using textbooks do *not* purchase and use the accompanying student manual.

Discussion Groups and Friends

Some of the best sources of test questions, yet often the most overlooked, are friends and fellow students. By talking with other students enrolled in the course or with students who have been enrolled in past semesters, you can formulate an excellent perspective of the types of questions and answers you should be looking for. Just as important is finding out what you might avoid.

Many students believe it's difficult to organize formal study groups. Some students simply prefer to work on their own. This strategy can be self-defeating. By organizing the questions and answers from a variety of sources, you are in an excellent position to compare yours with those of fellow students.

Compare this process to the pastime of trading cards, in which you collect as many cards as you can and simply trade off your extras to build up an even stronger set. Similarly, you find out what questions other students feel are important. You compare your answers with theirs to ensure that you haven't overlooked important information. Everyone comes out stronger than when he entered the game. Everyone is better prepared to ask and answer intelligent questions.

By studying in a group or with one other person, you will help to ensure that you

1. Structure a situation in which other people will encourage you to involve yourself in the study activities we have recommended.
2. Ask and answer questions that you believe are important and are likely to be found on your next exam.

3. Find questions that you hadn't predicted.
4. Refine your answers with additional information supplied by other students.
5. Put together practice tests.
6. Take practice tests.
7. Develop a more efficient and effective process of preparing for exams.

Instructors

Your instructor is the best source of information on forthcoming tests. Many students find it difficult to ask instructors what they believe is important. As we suggested earlier, most instructors are happy to tell you what they think is important. Give them a chance: Ask them!

Ask your instructor: "Could you specify the areas in which we should concentrate our studying?" "Are there particular topics which you feel we should devote more time to than others?"

Whatever you do, *don't* ask: "Are there any areas you feel are unimportant?" "Which of these chapters should we avoid, considering all that we have to study for this test?" If you ask such questions, the instructors may be so peeved that they will assign the encyclopedia. Most instructors believe that everything they teach is important. In trying to determine what is likely to be on exams, your goal is simply to persuade instructors to narrow down all the important things they have told you to a precise statement of what your exam will look like. If you are pleasant and thank your instructors for their help, you'll be way ahead of the game. You may even find out the exact format of the exam and which questions are most important.

The Result

Predicting exam questions is the most useful technique we have found in preparing students to learn the important concepts covered in their courses. Equally important, it helps them pass their exams with much greater ease. If you have followed our suggestions, you will have collected exam questions from

1. Your textbook chapters.
2. Your lecture notes.
3. Old exams.
4. Lists of questions in your textbooks.
5. Lists of questions in student manuals.
6. Discussion groups and friends.
7. Your instructor.
8. Lists of chapter objectives.

Once you have collected a good set of test questions, you will be better prepared to follow through with the procedures we suggest in the next section on tests.

Is the purpose of education to learn how to answer instructors' questions and pass tests? Yes and no! If you want to understand the experts and even go beyond them, it is important to be able to ask and answer the same questions that they believe are important. If you're realistic, you know you have to pass the requirements of the course. If you understand what your instructor wants, then you will learn a lot. If your instructor is less than adequate, then it is a matter of meeting his or her criteria and going on to better courses. There is no need to waste a lot of time in the process.

How can developing questions for class help me if I'm afraid of being called on in class? By preparing questions and answers and having practiced, you will be less afraid. It is natural to be scared if you are not prepared. Talk to yourself about the answers to questions your instructors are likely to ask in class. Once you have proven to yourself that you know the answers, you will be less fearful about your ability to answer similar questions in class. Language labs and discussion groups are useful places to begin to practice answering questions your instructors might ask in class.

If the fear comes from a general fear of having everyone look at you when you talk, go see what is available on campus in the way of assertiveness workshops or classes in verbal communications. If you ask around, you will find that there are some instructors who are very good at helping shy people become more comfortable speaking in groups.

Getting Started Developing
Questions and Answers

It is best to begin by practicing, predicting, and answering exam questions! Each week, count those questions and answers that you have collected from textbook reading, old exams, lecture notes, student manuals, discussion groups, classmates, and your instructors. To monitor how well you are doing, record the number of questions and answers you have for each class.

Action Review: Checklist for Successful Studying

Here is a list of guidelines that will help you to monitor your studying and your success at implementing the learning strategies we've described.

Y   N   NI*

1. ___ ___ ___ Do I, out of habit, use the SQ4R method for learning course material?

2. ___ ___ ___ Do I survey the reading first, ask questions, and then read to answer questions?

3. ___ ___ ___ Do I practice writing answers to questions and developing chapter summaries?

4. ___ ___ ___ Do I generate questions from lectures, textbooks, chapter summaries, student manuals, old tests, discussion groups, and chapter objectives?

5. ___ ___ ___ Have I asked my instructor what goals he or she has for the students in class?

6. ___ ___ ___ Do I keep a weekly record of the number of questions and answers I generate for each class?

*Y = Yes   N = No   NI = Needs Improvement

Chapter 7

Doing Well on Tests

Do you understand the relationship between making and taking practice tests and doing well on the instructor's tests?

Do you know that you can reduce nervousness during an examination if you feel free to write comments on the test?

Do you know that you can ask instructors about test items during the examination?

Guarantee Your Success on Tests

Here's a simple question. Have you ever taken an exam that didn't require you to answer questions? Exams in physical education, music, and other classes in which you perform are the rare exceptions. In most cases, your grades are determined by your answers to questions.

To do well in college, you have to be able to answer questions posed by your instructors in classes and on exams. That's why we've said that every time you read your course notes or texts, you should be looking for potential exam questions.

It makes sense that if you want to do well on your exams, you should practice taking exams. Spend your study time developing exam questions from notes and texts, then test yourself to see whether you can pass your exams.

The funny, and yet tragic, thing is that most students don't prepare for exams by taking practice tests. Most students prepare for exams by reading and rereading their notes, texts, and other sources of information. Have you ever known an instructor who asks you to come to an exam and read your notes or textbook to him? Absolutely not! Your instructors ask you to answer questions developed from their lecture notes and the textbook.

IF YOU WANT TO LEARN A LOT AND DO WELL ON TESTS, ALWAYS STUDY AS THOUGH YOU'RE PRACTICING TO TAKE A TEST.

Pretend you are the instructor. Make up exams just like the exams you believe your instructors will give you. Get your friends to quiz you on exams they have developed. Above all, develop a realistic means of learning to pass exams. Just as orchestras rehearse for concerts and football teams play practice games, prepare for exams by taking exams.

Preparing for Tests

Now that I have collected a good set of questions and answers, how can I make sure that I'll do well on the tests? Periodically, go through the questions you have generated to see whether or not you can still answer them. Avoid saying to yourself, "I know the answer to that one." Prove to yourself how brilliant you have become! *Orally and in writing, practice answering your questions.*

Review and Test

Using the questions you have collected, make up practice tests. Take practice tests under conditions as close as possible to actual test conditions. Then compare your answers with those you have generated from your textbooks, lectures, and so on.

Quiz Yourself

Here are some specific hints about making and taking practice tests, strategies for taking tests, and other useful exam preparation techniques.

When you quiz yourself orally from your notebook, cover up your answers with a blank sheet of paper. After answering your question orally, remove the paper and check to see how accurately you have answered your question. If you use cards, place your questions on one side and your answers on the other.

This system allows you to quiz yourself quickly by looking at your questions, providing written or oral answers, and then checking to see how well your quiz answers compare with your original answers.

Most students like this system because it gives them a central filing system of questions and answers. Rather than fumbling through lecture notes and textbooks, they go to their notebooks of questions and answers or their stacks of question cards and quiz themselves.

That sounds great for most students, but what about those of us who spend most of our time working problems in math and science? How can this technique help us? One of the most important insights that you can develop is recognition that success in a particular course is based upon solving specific problems, especially in mathematics, chemistry, physics, and engineering.

Reviews for science courses should be no different from reviews for other courses. You must practice working problems as similar as possible to those that will be found on your next exam. By recording sample problems on 4×6-inch cards or in notebooks, you will develop files of important problems that you should be able to solve if you wish to advance to more complex mathematical and scientific problem solving.

How about students in foreign language? Should they review in the same way? Yes, all students should review by practicing answering the important questions that are likely to appear on their next tests. Language students must maintain basic vocabulary and grammar skills if they wish to develop more complex language skills. By reviewing these areas, language students ensure themselves of continued involvement in the basics upon which more complex skills are built.

Making and Taking Practice Tests

Practicing the exact behavior you will be required to perform in a test situation not only prepares you to do well, but it also helps you to relax and build your confidence. After successfully passing practice tests, you are less likely to feel the uneasiness and tension about tests that may have accompanied your old study routines. You will know you have studied the right questions, and you'll sleep better for knowing you've studied correctly. Here is how to make and take practice tests:

1. Determine the amount of time you'll be given to take your instructor's exam; take practice tests over the same length of time. Taking tests under realistic time pressure is important. If you force yourself to do so, you'll feel more comfortable when you're in the actual testing situation.
2. Arrange the questions you've been accumulating from chapters, lecture notes, study groups, old exams, and other sources into practice tests.
3. If possible, test yourself on questions that are in the same format that the test will offer (multiple-choice, short essay, and so

on). This is where old tests come in handy. By practicing on old tests, you'll be more likely to be comfortable with your instructor's present test. Student manuals are also useful because they contain many questions in a variety of formats.

If all the questions you have developed from your notes and texts are short-answer questions and your test is going to be composed of multiple-choice questions, you needn't rewrite your questions to fit into a multiple-choice format. By quizzing yourself on your questions, you will be learning the information necessary to do well on your instructor's test, regardless of the format.

4. Take your practice tests under conditions as similar as possible to those under which you'll be tested. The classroom in which you'll be tested is the best place to take practice tests. If it is not available to you, make sure you practice in a room where you won't be bothered.

5. Try to answer your questions without referring to your books or other sources of information.

6. When attempting to answer questions for which you need more information, try to guess and make up things, as if you were in a real testing situation and trying to earn at least partial credit. This procedure forces you to take what you already know and determine what might be the answer rather than saying, "I just don't know!"

   Yes, this approach is known as "bulling" or being "creative," and it often makes the difference between an A and a B! Bulling is writing out an answer that makes sense to you, even though you don't remember exactly what was said in the textbook or lecture. You often know more than you think. An imaginative answer can be a good way to demonstrate your comprehension.

7. Once you have completed the test, compare your answers with those that you have in your own set of questions and answers. Use your textbooks and notes to refine your answers.

8. After noting the questions you have answered well and those in need of improvement, design a new test. Follow the same procedure that we have outlined in steps 1–7. Take the new test and continue repeating the steps until you think you have mastered all the questions and answers likely to appear on your instructor's test.

Weekly and Final Practice Tests

When you take weekly practice tests in each subject area, you'll find that exam panic and last-minute cramming are a thing of the past. Before each scheduled test, take a comprehensive practice test made up of sample questions from your weekly tests. You'll be pleasantly surprised at how much easier it is to pass your final practice test when you have been taking weekly tests.

Taking weekly tests allows you to master small amounts of information each week and then to put everything together in a final practice test just before you take the real thing.

The Advantages of Preparation Strategies

But isn't this strategy very time-consuming? It may appear so, but students who collect test questions and answers, take weekly practice tests (or quizzes), and take final practice tests spend far less time on irrelevant and wasteful studying. These students practice exactly what their instructors will require of them, "asking and answering intelligent questions."

Such students also obtain a more solid education. They remember what they have learned much better than students who "cram" for exams. Research into forgetting, done originally by Ebbinghaus and replicated many times over, shows that people quickly forget most of what they learn unless they review and rehearse the material.

We have assumed in our suggested study techniques that you want to pass tests well and obtain an excellent education. Your success in life after college is a function of what you can do, not of your grades. When you go to an attorney to have a contract drawn up, do you ask "What grade did you receive in contract law?" Or, if you have a pulled muscle, do you ask the physician about his or her scores on anatomy tests? No. You seek help or services on the basis of what people know and can do.

To obtain learning that lasts, each of us must apply the basic principles of learning. Otherwise, we end up with average grades but little knowledge.

Does making and taking practice tests reduce test anxiety? As we have noted, exam panic and last-minute cramming are unlikely to occur if you follow our suggestions for studying and exam preparation. What makes most people anxious is that they practice study behaviors and thought processes that are not similar to what is going to be required of them in the testing situation. If a person doesn't practice what is going to be expected of him, then it makes sense that he should be anxious. Especially when he walks into the test and sees that everything he studied only faintly resembles what is being asked of him. For example, if you are going to be asked to work chemistry problems on an exam, then you have to practice working problems as you prepare. If your English instructor is going to ask you to answer five short-answer essay questions about modern authors, then you have to practice writing answers to short-answer essay questions.

If you try to predict test questions and practice answering your questions, it is unlikely you will walk into an exam and find questions that are totally different from those you predicted. The minute you see that your instructor's questions resemble your own, your anxiety will decrease. The more you practice developing good test questions and practice taking tests, the faster you will see your test anxiety drop to a reasonable level.

Taking Your Instructors' Tests

Now that you know how to prepare for a test, let's make sure that you know how to relax and use your time wisely once you have the real test in your hands.

General Rules

1. Read the instructions to determine the types of questions you'll be expected to answer. Determine where you'll earn the most points. Don't spend a lot of time reading; just form a basic idea of how the test is set up, and plan your attack.
2. Divide your time to ensure that you schedule enough for all portions of the test. Otherwise, you'll devote too much time to the most difficult parts and wind up "choking" when you find that you won't be able to complete the whole test.
3. Before starting, determine whether or not answering the easier questions will earn you as many points as answering the more difficult questions. If so, complete the easy questions first. After answering them you'll have more confidence, and you will be able to pass on to the more difficult questions.
4. Make sure you understand what each question is asking. If the directions say, "Give several examples of . . . ," then do exactly that! Give instructors exactly what they ask for. Don't twist questions into something else.
5. If you don't understand a question or find it extremely difficult, place an X by it and move on to easier questions. You can come back later. This procedure saves time and prevents anxiety. Most important, you may find the answer hidden in other questions as you move through the test. Don't waste precious time trying to dig out the answers from the back of your brain. Expect the answer to come to you as you work on other items, just as you do when trying to recall a person's name. Relaxing and expecting the name to come to you in a few moments works better than struggling to remember.
6. Be sure to leave yourself a few minutes at the end of your exam to go over each section to see that you haven't forgotten to answer any questions.

Written Examinations

Written examinations tend to be of two types, long-answer essays and short-answer essays. A long-essay examination may ask you to answer only one question or at the most two, three, or four, depending on how much time you are given for the exam. Long-essay examinations ask you to "Trace the development of . . . , or "Explain and provide supporting evidence for each of the theoretical views . . . ."

At most schools, a short-answer essay exam will require that you answer five to ten essay questions. A short-answer essay question might ask you to "Briefly compare and contrast . . . , or "What are the major characteristics of . . . ."

Answering Short Essay Questions

The long essay questions may require an answer of several pages. The short-answer essay is more likely to require a third to a full page. The questions will ask you to:

Define each of the terms and concepts in a list.
Outline an experiment or study.
List the main points in favor of a procedure.
Give three criticisms against _____ .
Draw and correctly label a chart, graph, or structure (for example,
    a nerve cell).
Name the basic steps or stages in a process.

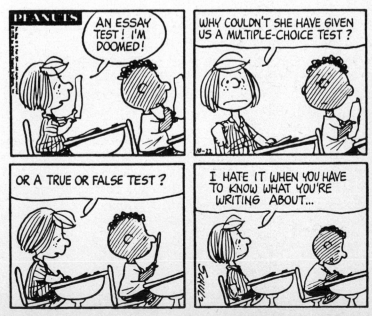

© 1970 United Feature Syndicate, Inc.

91

The answers to short essay questions will be brief sentences or lists that show you understand the main points. Be sure to highlight terms and concepts. Your job is to show the instructor in no more than several paragraphs that you understand the answer to the question. For ease of grading, instructors appreciate clear, legible answers.

Answering Long Essay Questions

OUTLINE ANSWERS

Outline your answer to a long essay question before writing it. In this way you will ensure that you include key ideas for which you will earn points from the grader. The procedure saves time in the long run. You can organize your answer and can be sure to include everything that is important. You will feel more organized when you begin to write and will have few uncertainties about whether you have included everything you should.

INTRODUCTION

Begin with several paragraphs that ask the most important questions or present the main ideas of your answer. It can help to pretend that you are writing a short article and need an interesting opening.

DEFINE TERMS

Define the terms that you use in your answer. Be sure to call attention to conflicting viewpoints or any uncertainties in your mind about the questions asked. This approach often clarifies for the instructor why you have answered the question in a particular manner.

USE SUBHEADINGS AND EXAMPLES

As you write, be sure to use subheadings for longer answers. Subheadings show you and the reader the organization in your answer. It is crucial to use examples to support your main points. You demonstrate that you really know what you are talking about if you can present examples to substantiate your position.

CONCLUSIONS

Summarize and draw conclusions. Be definite and positive. But note, do not include any new data, points, or examples in the conclusion! Add new questions, perhaps, but no new information.

POLISH ANSWERS

Above all, write legibly! After you have finished writing, pretend that you are the grader. Ask yourself, "Have I misread or misinterpreted the questions? What did I leave out? Have I made any careless mistakes?" Allot time at the end to polish your answers, add necessary points, and deal with more difficult questions that have puzzled you.

Answering Objective Questions

Never, never leave an answer blank, unless there is a penalty for guessing. If there is a penalty, guess only when you can eliminate at least half the possible options, two options where there are four in a multiple-choice question, for example.

Read objective questions carefully but answer them quickly. If the answer is not immediately obvious to you, check off a tentative answer and come back to it. Later items in the test often give clues to the answers in earlier items.

Contrary to the popular advice about never changing answers, *it can be to your advantage to change answers*. The research evidence shows that when students have prepared well for an examination, the number of students who gain by changing answers is significantly greater than the number of students who lose by changing answers. Be cautious about changing answers. But your second thought, if you have prepared well, may be more valuable than following a simple rule which is largely a myth.

ANSWERING MULTIPLE-CHOICE QUESTIONS

As you answer multiple-choice questions, always be sure to eliminate the obviously incorrect answers first. You will save considerable time and it will help to reduce anxiety about choosing the correct answer.

If after reading the question and all options the answer isn't immediately apparent, wait a second before you look at the options again. First, look at the question and try to develop an answer. Then look at the options to see if the answer isn't more apparent. Many students report this is a useful technique.

If a multiple-choice question doesn't make sense, read the question and each of the answers independently. By combining the question and the answers one at a time, you may figure out what the question is asking.

If the question is quite clear but none of the options seems to make sense, try combining the question with each option one at a time. Reading all four options together may create confusion. But by combining them independently with the question, one may stand out as correct.

When an "all of the above" option is available, be careful. Only when you can't eliminate one option will "all of the above" be correct. The same warning holds true for "none of the above." Unless you can find an obvious flaw in each answer, than "none of the above" is not your answer.

CHECK YOUR DIRECTIONS CAREFULLY!

Be sure that there is only one correct answer for each multiple-choice question. Few instructors develop multiple-choice questions with more than one correct answer. Be sure that your instructor isn't the exception.

Consider all options. Don't select the first one that looks good and forget to read the others. Sometimes instructors place a good, but not the best, option first to catch students who don't read each answer carefully. Read all options to make sure that you have chosen the best option.

Be cautious when an answer includes such absolute words as "every," "always," and "never." There are few situations in which something is always or never true.

Read and answer each question quickly. Look for key words and phrases such as "Which is *not* . . ." or "*According* to Skinner . . ." or "The *strongest* evidence. . . ." After you have answered all questions, go back and check to see that you have read them correctly. If you have time, reread them all. If not, reread those that you marked with X the first time through because you were unsure of your answers.

ANSWERING MATCHING QUESTIONS

Check to make sure you have read the directions for matching questions carefully. Sometimes students believe that matches are so obvious that they do exactly the opposite of what is asked. If the instructions say, "Match those that are different" or "Match those that are opposite," you'll feel rather foolish if you have spent a lot of time matching those that are similar.

A real time-saver is answering the easy ones first. This tactic reduces the chance of guessing incorrectly on more difficult matches.

ANSWERING TRUE-FALSE QUESTIONS

Never waste a lot of time pondering true-false questions. Many students have been known to waste major portions of test periods attempting to "solve" true-false questions, as if they were Chinese puzzles. If an answer isn't immediately apparent, don't become frustrated. Simply move on to the next question. Just one or two questions aren't worth that many points. They don't deserve the precious time that could be devoted to other, more important questions. The answers you don't recall on a true-false question may be recalled later in an essay question through a shrewd use of your imagination.

Questions You Didn't Think You Could Answer

Students are often amazed when we ask them to try answering questions and writing summaries after simply surveying a chapter. They say, "But I haven't read it yet!" Students then go ahead, do it, and find that their answers and summaries are fairly accurate, sometimes close to perfect. How do humans remember what they didn't know they knew? Stored in your brain, you have much information of which you are unaware. When you force yourself to come up with answers, you'll be amazed at how much you know!

We want you to remain humble, but we want you to be able to pull yourself out of jams by being creative. Go ahead and answer questions to which you have no immediate answers.

What can you do when you come to a question that baffles you? Try to remember that in your reading you're likely to have picked up some information that is relevant. Put down anything and you're likely to earn a few points, which is more than you'll have if you leave the answer blank. While taking the exam, you're likely to pick up some information related to the answer you need. If you can't figure out the exact answer, you can probably figure out an approximation. In math, for example, you may work out problems and come up with incorrect answers. You may not receive complete credit, but partial credit is surely better than a big zero.

Using your imagination takes practice and even a little confidence. It is not the most important study skill that we can recommend, but using your imagination can be valuable at times.

You Can Write Comments About the Test

If, in spite of all your excellent preparation, you are still a bit nervous about the test, then try imagining that written across the top of the test is the statement "Feel free to write comments about the test items."

Wilbert J. McKeachie, known for his research on ways to improve teaching, discovered that when this statement was printed at the top of tests, many students did better. The students who were helped most were those who had stronger than average fears of failing. An interesting result was that it didn't matter whether students actually wrote anything about the test! Just the presence of the statement was enough to improve the scores of students who had strong fears of failing.*

So, when you are taking a test, remember that you should *feel free to write comments about the test items!* If you believe that a question is poorly worded, then say so. But *also* go on to explain why and perhaps suggest a better wording. The whole purpose of the examination is to show that you know something about the subject. *Note:* If you have doubts about the instructor's allowing comments on the questions, then go ask!

Ask Questions During the Exam

Instructors know that their questions are not always clear. Sometimes the wording isn't as accurate as it should be. That's why most instructors will answer questions about test questions during exams.

Take advantage of this willingness. If there are one or two questions that just don't make sense, go ask the instructor such questions as: "I am a little confused by this question. Could you give me some assistance?" "The way this item is worded, couldn't there be several possible answers, this one and this one?" "I saw all the films but don't remember the one that this was covered in; can you give me any clues?"

If you are drawing a blank anyway, you have nothing to lose by seeing whether or not the instructor will give you some hints. He or she will not give you the answer, but a comment like "That item is from the chart at the end of Chapter 6" may give you the clue you need. Try asking. Asking the instructor for clues can be worth several extra points on every exam.

The Advantages of these Test-Taking Strategies

The strategies described in this chapter can improve your confidence by encouraging you to attack your tests in a reasonable and predictable manner. By using these techniques, you should achieve more points on any given test.

When taking tests, you will find that you don't make those stupid mistakes which make you want to kick yourself and ask, "Why didn't I use my brain?" You will read the questions carefully, plan your time well, determine the value of specific questions, and answer questions in ways likely to earn the maximum number of points. You will use test-taking behaviors that we most often observe in students who

*W. J. McKeachie, Donald Pollie, Joseph Speisman, "Relieving Anxiety in Classroom Examinations," *Journal of Abnormal and Social Psychology,* Vol. 50, No. 1 (January 1955), pp. 93–98.

comprehend their course material and do well on exams. In essence, you will be a more successful student and will still have time for friends!

Again we emphasize that students who use these techniques *seldom*

1. Misread the test questions and answer questions incorrectly.
2. Waste time on questions that stump them.
3. Waste time answering questions with information they know is irrelevant.
4. Run out of time and fail to complete the test.
5. Lose points as a consequence of changing their answers at the last minute.
6. Have difficulty answering questions that require them to "bull" a little.
7. Develop exam panic when a test appears more difficult than they had predicted.
8. Fail tests (they usually receive B or better).

Students who use these techniques report that they

1. Get better grades on tests.
2. Receive more points for answers than they would have predicted.
3. Feel more relaxed and confident while taking tests.
4. Feel confident that they haven't wasted their time while answering complex as well as simple questions.
5. Feel better organized while taking tests.
6. Seldom leave out important information in answers.
7. Are able to complete exams in the allotted time.
8. Get higher grades in their courses.

One Final Tip

It is not necessary to play the "suffering student" game. Learning can be pleasant. Studying for exams can be efficient if you use the principles we've just discussed. If you prepare well for exams, then the night before each exam you can relax and do one more very helpful thing: GET A GOOD NIGHT'S SLEEP!

Action Project: Review an "A" Essay Exam

1. ___ ___ ___ Get a copy of an "A" exam.
2. ___ ___ ___ Does the introduction include the key ideas that will be covered in the answer? Is it clear which questions will be answered in the essay?

3. ___ ___ ___ Are the terms and concepts clearly defined? Does it appear that the student got extra points for highlighting all the important terms and concepts?
4. ___ ___ ___ Does each paragraph have a central idea? Is the central idea supported and illustrated with examples to prove the point being made in the paragraph?
5. ___ ___ ___ Does the conclusion successfully summarize the main points made in the essay?

Action Review: Checklist for Success in Preparing for and Taking Tests

     Y   N   NI*

1. ___ ___ ___ Do I practice quizzing myself on possible test questions?
2. ___ ___ ___ Do I make up and take practice tests?
3. ___ ___ ___ Do I practice taking tests under conditions as similar as possible to those under which I will be tested?
4. ___ ___ ___ When I take tests, do I use the techniques suggested in this chapter?

*Y = Yes   N = No   NI = Needs Improvement

Chapter 8

Writing Excellent Papers: Using the Library Well

Do you know your first consideration when writing papers for instructors should be, "What questions am I trying to answer in this paper?"

Do you know how to use the library for research preparation?

Did you know that the reference librarian can help you discover reference sources?

Writing Papers for Instructors

The successful way to write papers closely parallels the steps you take in preparing for and taking tests. Begin by asking the following question when writing a paper for an instructor: "What important questions should I answer in this paper?"

For students willing to approach writing from this perspective, we have found the process to be less difficult and less time-consuming.

More important, their papers are precise, accurate, and well received by instructors. Here are the steps to follow in planning and preparing your papers.

Pick Your Topic

Pick the topic you find most interesting! Try to make it a topic that your instructor believes is important. By listening closely in class, you will often detect certain interest areas that are the instructor's favorites. Our students have found it best to choose topics that they and their instructors have enjoyed researching and reading about.

Instructors can supply bibliographies and other information about their favorite subjects. It may be helpful to talk with them after class or to make appointments to discuss your planned paper. Talking with the instructor will give you added insights on the advisability of writing in specific areas. It is also a good way to get to know your instructor.

When you have an assigned paper to write, our suggestion is that you prepare in advance by selecting at least three possible topics. Have a preferred topic, of course, but have several alternative topics that you would find interesting in case the first one proves to be unworkable. Make an appointment to talk with your instructor about your proposed topics. If you ask good questions during your discussion with the instructor, it is amazing how often the instructor will suggest many approaches, useful ideas, and key concepts to include which will almost outline how your paper should be written. During this discussion, your instructor can also warn you about certain problems to avoid and which issues are either too simple or too complicated to attempt in your paper.

Remember Your Audience

Always keep in mind that you are writing for an audience of one person, your instructor. You are not writing an article for the *Saturday Review* or for your school paper. You are not writing a paper which will be published as an article in a professional journal. Because your instructor is the person you are writing for, it is very important to take extra time to find out exactly what you need to do in your paper to get a good evaluation. If your instructor is vague or unwilling to talk with you about what you plan for your paper, talk to students who have taken the course in the past. Try to read papers that other students have written for this instructor to gain an idea about what was liked and disliked.

Ask Your Questions

Ask yourself, "What important questions should I answer in the paper if I wish to cover the topic adequately?" This attitude will help you determine whether your topic is too broad or too narrow. Too often students find that they would have to produce encyclopedias to cover all relevant questions adequately. If you limit yourself to a few important questions, you will be in a better position to relax as you do the research and writing.

Begin your paper by indicating that you intend to deal only with specific questions. Be humble and indicate that you recognize that there may be other significant questions, but that you have chosen to limit yourself to several high-priority questions.

What if my instructor says that I have missed the important question? What do I do then? This possibility is why we stress talking with your instructor to determine whether or not the questions that you think are important are those that the instructor would like answered.

What if I'm in a class of 200 and don't have access to the instructor or teaching assistant? You have several alternatives. Many schools provide students with a writing skills center. If you put into practice the recommendation in Chapter 3 about acquainting yourself with your campus, you should know where writing help is available. Take advantage of this useful *free* service! It is there for all writers, no matter what level they are at.

Go to the library. Find a *reference librarian.* Reference librarians are wonderful people to know. They can help you find sources of information you probably wouldn't think of. They know the library thoroughly and can be extremely helpful.

Skim through the most recent books and journals that deal with your topic. Even new books can be several years behind the times, so it is wise to go to journals that are more up-to-date. By looking at what the experts are doing, you are likely to get a better idea of the important questions currently being investigated.

Discuss your topic with students majoring in the subject. They may be aware of important questions that you have overlooked.

Once you have a list of good questions, the next step is to develop an outline of your paper.

Develop an Outline

Now that you have a list of questions, take a minute to develop an overall picture of your paper. Try outlining the paper. First will be your introduction. Sketch out one. An introduction is usually one or two paragraphs. It tells your instructor which important questions you intend to answer. By stating the main points you'll be making, you will focus the reader's attention. He or she will know what to look for. Don't worry about your introduction being perfect. It may change dramatically after you have answered your questions. Just sketch an introduction that will lead you in the right direction.

Next, list in order the questions you will be answering. Make sure your questions are listed in a logical sequence. The last part of your outline will be the conclusion. At this point, you haven't answered your questions, so you won't be in a position to draw any conclusions. Your outline will include:

I. A rough draft of your introduction
II. The body of your paper, the questions you intend to answer.
III. A statement that you will write a conclusion once you have found the answers to your questions.

Talk to Your Instructor

If after you have developed an outline, you wish to ensure that you are going in the right direction, make an appointment with your instructor. It will take the instructor only a few seconds to scan your outline to see if you are focusing on the important questions and issues. He or she may give you a few hints as to other questions you may wish to answer. Now, off to the library to find your answers.

How To Use Your Library Well

Libraries are wonderful places. In libraries you can discover extraordinary ideas, amazing information, and new worlds. You can find facts to support impressions you have, or data which disproves opinions you don't like. To have these experiences, it is highly important to know how to use a library.

To use your library well, as we've said before, feel free to ask the librarians for assistance. Librarians are paid to help students. More important, librarians want to be sure that every student gets the most possible from the library facilities. Whenever you have a question about using the library, don't be hesitant. Any question you have is a good one. The only poor question is the one you fail to ask.

Card Catalog and Microfiche

The card catalog is where you start in search of answers to your questions. Many libraries have converted the card catalog to a microfiche system. Microfiche is a piece of photographic film usually 4×6 inches. It contains information greatly reduced in size so it has to be magnified for reading. One microfiche sheet replaces dozens of catalog cards. It saves space, is cheaper to produce, and can be updated quickly. To use the microfiche, you sit down at a magnifier, insert the card, and find the items you are looking for.

Let's say your paper is going to be about nutrition and athletic performance. You've heard about high protein diets and carbohydrate loading and have seen ads for Gatorade. You've heard about professional athletes on vegetarian diets. How do you find out what the facts are?

With your question in mind, you'll probably want to start with the subject index. Libraries index their books in three ways: by *author*, *subject*, and *title*.

Use your imagination when looking through the subject index. Look under every topic you can think of—nutrition, dieting, physical education, health science, and so on. Make notes of book titles and authors and always write down the complete call number of the book. The call number is the library's code number which tells you exactly where the book is shelved.

If the entry for the book carries the statement "references" or "reference desk," you will not find the book in the open shelves. An instructor has probably placed the book on reserve so that no one can check it out of the library. If you go to the reference desk, they will probably let you have the book for several hours and, in some cases, for several days. At some libraries you can check out a reference book at closing time if you return it promptly first thing in the morning.

Periodical Index

After looking through the card catalog and microfiche, step over to where the library lists all of the periodicals it subscribes to. Most of your up-to-date information, especially scientific reports on research, appears in professional journals long before it is reported in books. Flip through the lists, looking for titles of journals that could contain articles related to your topic. For your paper you'd cover all the nutrition and physical education journals.

The journals of national professional groups are often titled *The American . . .* or *National Society of . . .* or *The Journal of the American. . . .* So be sure to look under "American," "National," and "Journal" in the alphabetical listings.

As you record call numbers for books and journals you will begin to see a pattern. The books and journals with relevant information are clustered in two or three places in the library. Now, by going to these sections, you will discover other books and journals that you didn't see in the catalog indexes.

Read first to get a general orientation. When you find useful data or passages you may want to quote in your paper, be very accurate in your recording. It can be very frustrating later when back at your typewriter you can't remember which author you quoted or if the statement in your notes is one of your own observations, rather than a quote obtained from an author. Most libraries have coin-operated photocopying equipment available. Save time by using it.

From the journal articles you will learn which authors are most highly regarded and most frequently cited as experts, and you will get clues about books to look for. Some professional journals publish book reviews of the latest books. You may learn about a book before the library purchases it. In such cases you may have to go to instructors in that area to see if any one of them has purchased the book and will allow you to borrow it.

From the books you will learn about which journals focus on your topic most frequently. You may learn about an older journal article that is exactly what you are after. You may discover, for example, that several articles on blood sugar and endurance have been published in medical journals. Thus, you have another area of information open up to you.

Reference Section

You still haven't used your library well, however, if you ignore a third source of useful information. It is the reference section. In the reference section you will find many resources, such as encyclopedias. Of most interest right now, however, is the *Reader's Guide to Periodical Literature*.

This index lists in alphabetical order the titles of articles published in the major popular magazines. If an article on nutrition and athletic performance has appeared in *Time, Saturday Review, Psychology Today, Sports Illustrated,* or *Runner's World,* the *Reader's Guide* will list it. Some physicians and scientific researchers publish directly in popular publications so don't discount magazines as a source of information. Besides, the information in them is usually easier to understand than it is in professional journals and books.

Use almanacs as well. Almanacs can sometimes provide historical facts, statistics, names, and dates not available in encyclopedias or other sources.

Use Other Libraries

Don't overlook other libraries in your area. Sometimes city or county libraries have books that the college libraries do not have. Other colleges in your area may have references which you cannot find in your own library on campus. You can use any library nearby, even the medical school library if there happens to be one in your vicinity. These other libraries may not allow you to check books out, but there is no problem in walking in and using any materials they have.

You'll soon discover that by having the questions in mind that you want to answer, you can quickly cut through the massive amount of material that could otherwise distract you. By reading to answer your questions, you save precious hours that might otherwise be lost in meandering around, wondering how much you should include in your paper.

Writing Your Paper

Write Your Answers

Gathering your information is likely to be the most time-consuming part of writing the paper. Once you have the necessary information, it is time to write the answers to your questions.

Write the answers to your questions as precisely as possible. Be brief. Don't include irrelevant information that clouds the issue. Make your point, back it with sufficient examples and data, and leave it at that.

Give precise references to your information sources in footnotes and in your bibliography. Provide all the information a reader needs to go to the specific publication and find the exact pages referenced.

Answers to questions are more believable when they are precise and well documented. Let your reader know that you've done research on the answers. Quote experts in the field. The more authoritative your examples, the better you will be able to convince your reader. But don't overdo it. Several good examples are all that you need to prove your point.

Brief accurate quotations are more effective in supporting your points than lengthy quotations or your statements about what other people have said. Brief quotations, figures, and specific facts are more persuasive than vague generalizations.

Arrange Your Answers

Once you have written your answers, arrange them in order so that they build upon one another. Your next task is to connect them by writing the minimum amount of material between each answer. These transitions from answer to answer should be brief.

Rewrite Your Introduction

Now that you have answered your questions and built the body of your paper, you are ready to rewrite your introduction. Many students try to start writing their paper by producing a perfect introduction for their outline. This is a mistake.

Once you have answered your questions, you'll be much better prepared to state exactly what your paper does and does not do. You may have found that several of the questions you originally thought you would answer were less important than other questions you discovered while researching your paper.

Write Your Conclusion

Your conclusion summarizes the major points you have addressed in your paper. You shouldn't include any new data, examples, or information. You may wish to point out that your paper raises further questions which need to be answered at a later date. Essentially, your summary shows how all the pieces fit together to prove a particular point. If the answers to your questions lead to a logical conclusion, then you should draw that conclusion and leave it at that.

The Steps So Far

1. Determine which questions you will answer in your paper.
2. Develop an outline for your paper. Write an introduction describing the intent of your paper and the questions you will answer.
3. Ask your instructor to scan your outline.
4. Answer each question as precisely and authoritatively as possible. Provide examples to support your position.
5. Document your sources in footnotes and a bibliography.
6. Put your answers in sequence so that they build upon one another.
7. Provide transitions from answer to answer.
8. Rewrite your introduction.
9. Write your conclusion.

Rewrite Your Paper

After you write your first draft, make an appointment to go over it with your instructor. Most instructors are willing to help you and will give you good feedback about whether you are ready for the typewriter or need to do more research.

Revising is where the real writing of any paper takes place. Most writers produce several rough drafts before attempting their final version. Plan from the beginning to produce a rough draft which you will then revise into your final copy. This way you can produce your first rough draft much more quickly and won't be wasting time going back trying to edit, correct typing mistakes, and such as you write out or type your first draft.

When you are in a position to rewrite your paper, you should

1. Have your instructor look over your rough draft.
2. Make sure you have clearly indicated which questions you will answer.
3. Check to see that your transitions flow smoothly from answer to answer.
4. Vary the length of your sentences. Most of the writing in journals and research books is composed of long, complicated sentences. Such sentences are typical of the way many academics think and talk. Long sentences do not make interesting reading, however. On the other hand, you don't want to make your writ-

ing style too simple. The best approach is to mix both long and short sentences.

5. Correct any grammatical, punctuation, or spelling errors.
6. Rewrite or refine any answers.
7. Finish the paper with concluding comments and remarks. *Include in this section statements about what you learned in the process of writing the paper.* State why writing the paper was a valuable experience for you. Also include questions, if any, that writing this paper has raised in your mind.

Good Effort and Learning

The grade given for a paper is influenced by three questions in the back of the instructor's mind:

1. Did the student put good effort into this paper or was it written with the minimum possible effort?
2. Did the student learn anything or is this paper just a collection of words?
3. Is the paper original or has it been plagiarized?

If you can arrange to do so, glance through a large number of papers. Certain quick impressions will begin to emerge. Some students turn in papers that show very little effort. You don't have to be an instructor to see that such students are trying to get away with the absolute minimum commitment of time, effort, and involvement.

INSTRUCTOR REACTION:	Disgust
STUDENT LEARNING:	None
GRADE:	D to C −

Some students do more work, but they lack involvement with the topic. Their approach is to check out all the books they can on the subject, sit down the night before the paper is due, and put together lists of quotations: "In 1937, C. S. Johnson said . . . . His view was criticized by Smith who said . . . , by Brown who said . . . , by Jones who said. . . . But then in Eggland's 1949 book. . . ."

INSTRUCTOR REACTION:	Ho-hum, a collection of secondhand ideas
STUDENT LEARNING:	Minimal, shows no thinking
GRADE:	C to B −

Once in a while, a student will copy long passages from a book or article and will turn in the paper without mentioning the author's name or the source of the quotations. Does this approach succeed? Rarely. An article written by an expert on a subject is not like a paper written by a student who is attempting to learn a subject. And, frankly, most instructors can spot the style and point of view in the paper as having come from a certain author.

INSTRUCTOR REACTION: Plagiarism
STUDENT LEARNING: Zero, tried to cheat
GRADE: F

It's human nature to consider taking shortcuts, but some efforts to save time involve high risks. The probability is high that the payoff will be the opposite of what is desired. That's why asking and answering questions works so well. An instructor reading your paper can see that your work is *original*, that you put *good effort* into it, and that you have *learned* something. Remember, an experienced instructor will usually be able to recognize exactly what you do or don't do in preparing your paper.

Grammar, Spelling, and Neatness

One final set of suggestions is important. Determine whether your instructor requires that papers by typed. You can safely assume that the instructor prefers it, for most instructors do. If you can't type, consider taking a typing class. In any case, typing is easy to learn and is one of the best investments you can make in self-improvement. (*NOTE:* Your school may offer a credit course in typing. If so, you can not only learn a valuable skill, but you may even earn credit toward your degree as well!)

Hand-written papers are difficult to read. They slow down the instructor and cause eye strain. Your instructor reads hundreds of articles, books, and papers every year. It is a sign of consideration to present your writing in the most readable form. Make your typed copy as professional as possible. Use clean white paper, double-space the lines, and make a minimum number of corrections on the typed copy.

Always be careful to follow any directions your instructor gives for footnotes, bibliographies, references, or other requirements. There is nothing worse than devoting hours to a paper only to have it returned as incomplete. The consequences of failing to follow directions can be costly.

It can be a pain in the neck to follow the requirements assigned by your instructors. It may be one of the small sacrifices you have to make as a student. You may be dismayed to find that what your instructor wants for the form of a paper contradicts what your English instructor taught you to do. In the end, however, you'll probably find out that there's a good reason for your instructor's request. Go along with the suggestions and you will usually be better off, both in the grade you receive and in the level of your blood pressure after completing the paper.

Above all, make sure that your spelling is accurate. Use a dictionary whenever you are in doubt. If you find that you have serious problems in this area, you will be wise to make an arrangement with someone to check your paper for spelling and grammatical mistakes. Regardless of the quality of your ideas, there are few things that bother instructors more than poor spelling and bad grammar.

It has been shown in several studies that instructors usually grade papers higher when the papers are neat and clean and when they include good spelling and good grammar. *A word to the wise:* Look sharp, at least on paper.

NOTE: Always keep a copy of your paper. The original could get damaged or lost. Some instructors keep papers. Play it safe. Make a copy for yourself before turning in the original.

Two Important Tips

In working with college students, there are two things we have observed that will help any writer. First, when you write, read aloud what you have written. So very often students fail to pick up obvious mistakes because through silent reading they miss things that would be obvious to them were they to read their papers aloud.

Second, after you have written a rough draft, try to get someone else to read the paper to see if it makes sense. Listening to feedback from another person regarding your writing is often painful. But it is more painful to hear those same remarks from your instructor. Do the same for your friends. Read their papers. Learn to be a better writer from analyzing the mistakes of others. As you exchange information about one another's writing, be pleasant and give constructive help. Try to encourage one another.

Make Sure Your Work Is Your Own

Many students unintentionally find themselves in a tremendous bind as a result of not knowing exactly what plagiarism is and is not. Below is a discussion of plagiarism written by our friend and colleague John Gardner of the University of South Carolina. After reading John's description, we're sure you'll be well aware of how to make use of information produced by other people without getting yourself in a bind.

Statement on Plagiarism*

Plagiarism: This has a number of different meanings. It is theft of knowledge from another person, because it means that you are submitting the

*This statement is an excerpt from the original authored by Dr. John N. Gardner of the University of South Carolina in collaboration with Professor Francis Marion Nichols, Winthrop College, Department of History, 1969.

work of another person as if it were your own. Thus, it means failure to acknowledge borrowed ideas, words, phrasing, or data. More specifically, this means using the words, ideas, etc. of another person without so indicating by means of footnoting and/or quotation marks. Plagiarism occurs in a number of circumstances:

1. When the student copies an original source *intentionally* and does not give proper credit for the real authorship.
2. When a student *unintentionally* copies from an original source and does not give proper credit.
3. When a student directly quotes words from the writing of another without using quotation marks and footnoting.
4. When a student directly quotes from the writing of another and uses quotation marks but does not use a footnote.
5. When the student fails to paraphrase in his/her own words and when he/she does not footnote paraphrased material. Paraphrased material must be footnoted because, even though the words are yours, the original ideas are not.

Examples:

In order to better help you understand what constitutes plagiarism please read *carefully* the three examples below and note the explanations for each.

I. ORIGINAL QUOTATION

"Local color is a much-abused element in modern writing, but its desirability is only too strongly shown in this volume. Jay spends over two years in Spain, yet no account is given of the nature of the court from which he sought recognition; he is elected president of Congress when but three days a member, but scarcely a hint is given of the reasons for so astonishing a selection. A similar mistake is the introduction of the names (not quite the personalities) of men not today known to the average reader, without a word to explain their positions or characters or even their nationality. Thus Marbois, Vergennes, Luzerne and Gerard are spoken of with the same familiarity that we are accustomed to use in mentioning Washington, Jefferson, Hamilton or Jay."[2]

II. DIRECT PLAGIARISM

"Local color" is a much-abused element in modern writing, but its desirability is only too strongly shown in this book. Jay spends over two years in Spain, yet no account is given of the nature of the court from which he sought recognition; he is elected president of Congress when but three days a member, but no evidence is given of the reasons for such a selection. A similar mistake is the introduction of the names of

[2]Henry Mammon Neill, review of *John Jay* by George Pellew, *Political Science Quarterly*, Vol. 5 (1890), p. 545.

men not known today to the average reader, without a word to explain their positions or characters or even their nationality. Thus Marbois, Vergennes, Luzerne, and Gerard are spoken of with the same familiarity that we are accustomed to use in mentioning Washington, Jefferson, Hamilton or Jay.

III. INDIRECT PLAGIARISM

A much-abused element of current literature is local color, this is shown only too strongly in this volume. Jay spends more than two years in Spain, but there is no account in the book describing the court from which he sought recognition. No reasons are given for his astonishing selection as president of Congress, when he had been a member only three days. A mistake of a similar nature is the introduction of the names of men not known to today's average reader, such as Marbois, Vergennes, Gerard, and Luzerne, without an explanation of their position, character, or even their nationality.

Explanation of examples: Example I is a direct quotation. This is a certain guarantee to avoid plagiarism, i.e. by quoting the original source and so indicating by placing the quotation in quotation marks and concluding by footnoting. Quotes of this length should also be indented and single-spaced if your text is double-spaced.

Example II is one of direct plagiarism in which the direct quotation above in Example I is copied *verbatim* (with the exception of a few words). This is plagiarism because no credit is given to the original author by means of quotation marks and a footnote. This means that the student is passing off the work of another as his/her own.

Example III shows us the case where the student has merely rephrased the original quotation. The ideas and their order of expression are unchanged, and he/she gives no credit for this borrowing of ideas. Thus, even though he/she has not copied directly and *verbatim*, he/she has still plagiarized.

The way to have avoided plagiarism in Examples II and III would have been to have footnoted in both cases and used quotation marks when appropriate.

REMEMBER: If you are in doubt as to whether you are plagiarizing, do two things:

1. See your instructor for guidance.
2. Footnote and use quotation marks!

Action Project: Researching Research

1. Go to the library.
2. Locate *The World Book Encyclopedia.*
3. Read the chapter on "How To Do Research" in volume 22.

Action Review: Checklist for Success in Writing Papers and Using Your Library

	Y	N	NI*	
1.	—	—	—	Do I write papers using the question and answer format?
2.	—	—	—	Have I asked the reference librarian for suggestions about where to look for information?
3.	—	—	—	Do I use the card catalog and microfiche to track down good reference sources?
4.	—	—	—	Do I get up-to-date information from professional journals?
5.	—	—	—	Do I use the *Reader's Guide* to learn about useful magazine articles?
6.	—	—	—	Do I use other libraries in the vicinity?
7.	—	—	—	Are my quotes and references accurate?
8.	—	—	—	When the rough draft is completed, do I ask the instructor to look it over and give me suggestions for improvement?
9.	—	—	—	Do I check to ensure that my grammar and spelling are correct?
10.	—	—	—	Is my written work clean and readable?

Suggested Reading

Strunk, William, Jr., and E. B. White, *The Elements of Style* (New York: Macmillan, 1979). This book can be valuable to any person wanting to improve the quality and clarity of their written communications. Buy a copy and hang on to it. This little book is the best book in print on how to use good grammar, punctuate correctly, and write clearly.

Turabian, Kate L., *Student's Guide for Writing College Papers*, 3rd ed. (Chicago: University of Chicago Press, 1976).

*Y=Yes N=No NI=Needs Improvement

PART THREE

Doing Well in School and Life

C h a p t e r 9

Erroneous Beliefs
About Instructors

*Do you know that many students have
erroneous beliefs about instructors?*

*Do you know that unrealistic expectations about
instructors can make you angry and disappointed?*

*Do you know how to change unrealistic
expectations about instructors?*

Do You Make Erroneous Assumptions About Your Instructors?

When you accept complete responsibility for learning as much as possible from your instructors, you're on the right track. You will get more than your money's worth from school. If, however, you assume that your instructors are responsible for your learning everything you want to know, you may become disappointed with your schooling.

A candid appraisal of instructors and of your assumptions about instructors will help you understand why many of your assumptions are not justified. When we teach, we sometimes ask students to list their assumptions and expectations about instructors. Then we compare the assumptions and expectations with reality. In the pages that follow, you will be able to discover which of your beliefs and expectations about instructors are erroneous and which are realistic.

In front of each statement you'll find two spaces. Check off whether or not you believe the statement.

We want you to learn about myths* which may be affecting your assumptions of what your instructors should be like. Most important, we want to encourage you to stop letting erroneous beliefs set you up to feel angry, disappointed, and discouraged.

After you have read through the myths, we'll talk about predictable conflicts between teaching styles and learning styles, some successful ways to gain as much as possible from a variety of different types of instructors, and what to avoid doing to alienate your instructors.

Myths about Instructors

Yes   No

___ ___ Myth No. 1   Most college instructors are trained in how to be effective instructors.

Reality: Colleges usually assume that a person with a graduate degree in a subject should be able to teach it. Yet few of your college instructors have received formal training in how to be effective teachers. New instructors learn how to teach through trial and error during their early years as instructors and assistant professors. Very few instructors receive training for one of their major responsibilities—TEACHING!

___ ___ Myth No. 2   All of your instructors will be interesting lecturers and devote considerable effort to making the course stimulating and motivating.

Reality: Most of your college instructors would like to be interesting, stimulating, and motivating lecturers. But you will find that your instructors vary widely in their ability to maintain your interest. Some of your instructors will be downright boring and uninteresting regardless of how hard they try to maintain your interest. These instructors may still be excellent at presenting the information you want to learn. They are just not entertainers.

___ ___ Myth No. 3   Your instructors will always be well prepared for each class you attend.

Reality: Most of your instructors will be well prepared for each class. Regardless of how well your in-

*As used in this chapter, the term "myth" means "A collective opinion, belief, or ideal that is based on false premises or is the product of fallacious reasoning" (Funk & Wagnalls' *Encyclopedic College Dictionary*).

structors plan, sometimes a class won't work out as well as they hope. Sometimes, instructors' commitments and personal lives get in the way of their planning. They may come to class poorly prepared. Some of your instructors may even get to the point where they feel too confident and do little or no planning.

Myth No. 4　Every instructor will take a personal interest in you.

Reality:　Some instructors will want to get to know you as a person and will devote a lot of time to you. They will enjoy talking with you after class, around campus, in their offices, and at social or athletic events. Some instructors, however, are so busy that they just don't have much time for students. They are too busy with academic responsibilities, research, writing for publication, teaching classes, and various professional activities to have much time for anyone—even their own families. Still others are very private people. They prefer to keep things strictly on a teacher–student basis and do not see that personal interest in students has a place in the classroom.

Myth No. 5　University and college instructors have little personal interest in students and should not be asked for assistance if a course is too difficult.

Reality:　Many students are so awed by having an instructor who has been transformed into a prestigious noun such as "doctor" or "professor" that they assume such an instructor will have little interest or concern for a lowly student. Impressive titles and offices heaped with books and papers do tend to create distance between instructors and students, but most instructors are available and enjoy contact with students sincerely motivated to learn. Unfortunately, many students who could use help in a course do not seek assistance because of erroneous beliefs about instructors' attitudes.

Myth No. 6　Your instructors want all ideas challenged and want students to present their opinions and views during class.

Reality:　Many of your instructors will seek as much appropriate and useful student input as possible. A small proportion of your instructors will have little or no interest in students' opinions and views. Other instructors will feel that they have limited time in which to present vast amounts of important information. These instructors are often rather dedicated individuals who don't

117

wish to offend students but very often discourage student input so as to maintain their schedules. For such instructors, getting through the course material is more important than letting students express views.

Myth No. 7 The instructor's coverage of the course material will be nonjudgmental, unbiased, objective, and comprehensive.

Reality: Many instructors use teaching as a way to advocate and promote their personal perspectives on their subject. They tend to play up why their approaches, conclusions, and methods are correct while the views and teachings of some other people in the field are wrong. A few instructors make it clear in their reactions to questions about opposing views or the works of certain people that such ideas or works are not worthy of attention.

Myth No. 8 Instructors want you to accept obediently everything they say without reservation and be able to regurgitate accurately on exams the truths they've taught.

Reality: Most instructors have two goals. One is for you to understand the basic facts and concepts in the field or subject being taught. The other is for you to learn to think for yourself. Once you gain a sense of these two goals, you can learn the content of the course and at the same time question basic assumptions.

Myth No. 9 Your instructors will be pleasant people.

Reality: Many of your instructors will be people who have entered the teaching profession because they enjoy having a positive effect on other people. These instructors will often be pleasant to be around and have a profound effect on their students. A small proportion of your instructors will be neither pleasant nor unpleasant. These instructors will simply be there to help you learn. A very small proportion of your instructors will be irritable, unpleasant, and bores to be around. If you are asking the question, "Do I like this instructor?" you are asking the wrong question. The right question is, "Does this teacher know the subject well enough to teach me something?"

Myth No. 10 Your instructors will be able to answer all of your questions about the subject.

Reality: Most instructors see education as an ongoing process for themselves as well as for their students. Being well educated includes learning what you don't know. Being well educated is to discover that some answers are partially true or only correct in certain circumstances.

Would you rather have an instructor who can give you what seems to be a definite, correct answer about everything or one who says, once in a while, "I don't know," and then suggests a way to find the answer?

One of the results when you ask good questions and learn what the answers are is that you eventually run out of people who can answer your questions. Questions that no one can answer well are the forerunners of new knowledge, scientific advances, and exciting career directions.

Myth No. 11 Your instructors will know more than you.

Reality: If you've had a thirst for knowledge for many years, read a lot, and learned from life's experiences, you may find that you know more about some things than the instructor does. As disappointing as this may be to you, the fact is that you may be too advanced for the class. If so, is that a legitimate excuse for being angry at the instructor or the school?

One of the signs of having an educated heart as well as an educated mind is that you can handle those times when you discover that someone with an advanced degree knows less about a topic than you. And if you think you understand the topic so well, how about taking your turn as a teacher? Are you ready for that?

Myth No. 12 Your instructor must have firsthand experience to be able to teach a subject well.

Reality: In trade schools, experience is essential. There are many courses, however, where the sniping comments such as "How can he know, he's never been there," serve only to rationalize not listening. An instructor in management can teach many practical ideas without ever having owned or run a business. A person can teach child development well without having had children. A psychologist can teach about mental disturbances without having been a mental patient. History and geography teachers can teach well without having "been there."

Firsthand experience is very useful but not essential. In fact, many people with experience don't know how to teach what they do. Have you ever tried to learn from Granny exactly how she makes that special dessert all the family loves? Or ask Uncle Ned exactly how he knows which wood to use? Asking "has the instructor had firsthand experience?" is asking the wrong question. Asking, "can this instructor teach well?" is a better question.

Your Attitudes Affect Your Success in School

When we talk to students about the myths versus the realities of college instructors, we hear hilarious, impassioned, and periodically bitter stories of students' feelings for and against instructors. There is no question that your instructors' personalities and teaching behaviors will have a profound impact on your attitude toward learning and your performance in college. *What does all this mean for you?*

The reality of going to college is that you'll attend courses taught by instructors with just about every personality characteristic imaginable. You'll attend courses taught by highly competent instructors and less competent instructors. That is simply the way things work.

What is important for you is that *you can make your attitudes about instructors work for you or against you! You can attempt to get the most possible out of every course, regardless of your instructors' personalities or levels of competency. Or you can go around complaining and moaning about your instructors and blame them for why you are not learning anything! It is all up to you!*

Action Project: Dispelling a Myth

The way you react when an instructor doesn't live up to your expectations about what a good instructor should be like determines how good an education you get. When you are disappointed, do you get mad at the instructor and the school, or do you find a way to make the course turn out well for yourself?

1.   Look back through the list of myths, select one that you answered "yes" to, and challenge yourself to dispel that myth. Focus your attention on the reality of how things are with your instructors by answering these questions:

Are my thoughts and beliefs about each instructor based on actual experience, or do they come from past experiences with other teachers and statements made by other students?

Why is it reasonable and legitimate for instructors to be as they are even though I may be disappointed or upset?

Can I learn something from an instructor who is less than ideal— who has weaknesses, flaws, and limitations?

2. How could you go about changing the habits and attitudes that are based upon your assumptions? What would be the benefit to you?

3. Set a goal to dispel a myth in which you believe. Describe what you would do on a daily basis for the next month to demonstrate to yourself how erroneous your assumptions have been.

4. A month from now, come back to this space and write in exactly what it is that you did over the past month to change your habits and attitudes. How did you dispel the myth?

Additional Challenge

What are some myths that instructors have about students? How do you handle a situation in which an instructor has expectations or beliefs about what you should be like and you are not able to live up to them?

Chapter 10

Resolving Conflicts Between Teaching Styles and Learning Styles

Do you know that you may be handicapping yourself with the attitude "If only other people would change, my world would be a better place for me"?

Do you know that certain conflicts between students and instructors are predictable?

Do you know that difficulties in school frequently stem from a mismatch between an instructor's teaching style and students' learning styles?

Do you know that your attitudes about instructors can work for you or against you?

Can you distinguish between different teaching styles and adjust your learning style accordingly?

Predictable Conflicts between Teaching and Learning Styles

Research into teaching effectiveness led psychologists to the questions: "Why do some students do well with one instructor but not another?" "Why do instructors do well with some students but not with others?"

Efforts to answer these questions uncovered a simple but relevant factor: *The way some people teach doesn't always match up with the way other people learn.*

Based on the research and on our own experiences, here are some differences between students and instructors which lead to some predictable conflicts.

Auditory Versus Visual Styles

Some people learn best by listening. Information doesn't stick well unless they hear it. Other people learn best by reading. They must see something before they believe it and remember it.

What is your natural preference?

Do you remember best what is said to you or what you read?

Do you prefer television or newspapers as your source of news?

Would you rather hear an expert talk on a subject or read what the expert has written?

If you have some spare time, would you rather sit around talking with people or go to the library and read?

If someone sends you a note setting up a time to get together, does the date really register with you or must you also hear it said out loud?

If you are working with a group of people and there is some discrepancy between the written guidelines and the verbal instructions, which do you tend to believe?

Was reading the college catalog your main way of learning about your program and classes or did you merely skim the catalog and go see an advisor, who told you everything you needed to know?

Everyone learns both ways, of course. We are not talking about an either/or situation. Yet the differences between people are sometimes extreme enough to cause some basic problems. If you have a visual learning style, you operate mainly on the basis of what you read. You may have some difficulty with a verbal-auditory instructor who believes that merely telling people what to learn and know is sufficient.

If you have a verbal-auditory style, you will probably do well with an instructor who says everything to learn and do. You may have some difficulty with a visually oriented instructor who hands out a written statement about what to do to pass the course and who doesn't want to discuss it—who assigns textbook material and outside readings that are never discussed in class.

If you learn best visually, then you may be in trouble with an instructor who doesn't use handouts or doesn't write much on the blackboard. You may have problems with instructors who use class discussion as a teaching tool.

As you will see at the end of the chapter there are several solutions possible for any of these problems. Before getting into ways of resolving such difficulties, however, we want to go through more of the predictable conflicts between teaching styles and learning styles.

Intellectual Versus Metaphoric

Increased knowledge about the functions of the brain have changed the old views about how your brain operates. Years ago, students learned that their brains (the cerebral cortex) had two halves. These were referred to as the two hemispheres of the brain, and one of the hemispheres was understood to be dominant over the other.

The newer view is that instead of conceptualizing what is inside your skull as a brain with halves, it is more accurate to think of yourself as having two brains. The *left* brain is where your speech center develops. Speech development is closely related to "handedness." With some exceptions, if you are right-handed your speech centers develop in your left brain. Once this occurs, many related functions develop in the left brain. Here is where you remember words, use logic, and think analytically and objectively about the world. The left brain makes possible your ability to think rationally and unemotionally. The left brain thinks in a linear fashion, following a logical sequence to an end point. It is time oriented. It makes intellectual skills possible.

The right brain carries your memory for music. You think visually, emotionally, and irrationally in the right brain. It is the source of creativity and intuition. Right-brain thinking follows emotional logic. Using it, you can visualize and think in patterns, jumping from one spot in a pattern to another without apparent logic or reason. Although it has no speech center, the right brain can produce a few words that go along with strong emotions or music. Stroke patients who have lost their powers of speech can, when upset, still swear. They can, when remembering a childhood melody such as "Twinkle, Twinkle Little Star," recall a few of the words. The right brain is your metaphoric mind. It focuses on the pattern and emotional truth of things with images which are like what is being experienced. For example, a woman trying to tell her group what it was like to live with her husband said, "With him what I get is like a long drought with an occasional thunderstorm; what I need is a gentle rain." Telling a child he "eats like a pig" is a metaphoric statement.

If you tend to be a left-brain person, then you will be well matched

124

to an instructor who gives you a thorough, unemotional listing of facts, data, analytic explorations, hypotheses, logic, evidence, numbers, definition of terms, and rational conclusions.

If you tend to be left-brained and get an instructor who teaches in a right-brained way, you may find the course a bewildering experience. You may have experienced the instructor as weird, too emotional, and a bit nutty. After all, there must be something wrong with a management instructor who reads poetry in class. And isn't it amazing how some students really enjoy it? They actually believe this is a great teacher and a wonderful class.

If you tend to be right-brained with a left-brained teacher, the course will be painful for you. You'll feel like a thirsty person reaching for a glass of water only to discover that it is filled with sand. Something in you will be crying out, "Where is the heart? Why is there no life to this?" You may wonder, "Where is the humor, the drama, the excitement? These facts all seem to make sense, but what can I do with them? Why are we painstakingly dissecting every tree and plant when I want to experience the rich sweep of the forest?"

The solution to this sort of conflict, as we've stated before, is to *avoid indulging in the attitude "If only other people would change, my world would be a better place for me."* You can try to find someone (perhaps even the instructor) who can translate the material presented to you into a form you can understand better. More importantly, however, we recommend that you work at gaining more use of your other brain.

Adopting a different style may not be easy at first, but it does give you a chance to add another dimension to yourself. And isn't that what you're in school for? **REMEMBER:** *You do not have to give up your more natural and preferred way of thinking, feeling, and talking.* What you can do is add more to what you already have. We'll cover more on this in the section on the survivor personality. In Chapter 13, we show how a person can benefit from using both brains well.

Friendly Versus Distant

Imagine your instructor stopping you as you leave the classroom and saying, "I liked the paper you turned in last week and want to talk with you about it. Do you have time to come and have a cup of coffee with me?"

How would you react? Would you be pleased and eagerly accept the invitation? Or would you draw back and make up an excuse to get away?

Just as it has been throughout your life, instructors and students vary considerably in how friendly they want to be and how much distance they need to have. A friendly, extroverted instructor enjoys after-class contact with students. He or she will ask students to coffee, to evenings at the pizza house to talk and drink, and perhaps even to parties where the instructor lives. If you are similarly friendly and enjoy that, then you are going to have a wonderful year.

If you are a more introverted person, however, you may suffer a bit from personal attention and closeness. You would much rather have a quiet, tactful instructor who respects your need to be left alone. Such an instructor understands how embarrassing it is to be called on to talk in class or to be openly praised for getting a high score on an exam.

On the other hand, if you are a basically friendly person with a more introverted instructor, you may find it puzzling to have him or her pulling away from you after class. After all, what are instructors for if not to be available for students? Yet your inclination to want to be friendly and chat a while may cause the instructor to stare at you and make an excuse to get away quickly. Then, after that, you get the feeling that you are being avoided.

The solution we recommend was covered in Chapter 9. If an instructor doesn't live up to your expectations about what an instructor should be like, then question your "shoulds." When reality is inconsistent with your beliefs and erroneous expectations, then what is the best solution?

"External" Versus "Internal" Learning Styles*

In Chapter 2 we looked at how attitude differences described as "external" and "internal" affect your success in school. These same attitudes influence how you learn as well. Some "external" learners are only open to believe information that comes from an authority or expert. Information or suggestions from other sources can't be trusted as accurate. If you prefer to get the guidance from expert sources and your instructor enjoys being an expert, then you have a good match.

The more you need an instructor who tells the class exactly what to learn and then tests the class on how well they've done as told, then the better you will do with this type of instructor. If you need clear guidelines from instructors but take a course from someone who gives little clear direction, you may flounder a while. You may be sitting in class waiting for the instructor to tell you what the answer to a problem is, only to have him or her ask the class, "What do you think?" And after waiting for the class to get through talking, the instructor may refuse to say what the right answer is. He or she may say, "You may be right," or "There is some truth to that."

---

*Adapted from Julian Rotter in "Generalized Expectancies for Internal Versus External Control of Reinforcement," *Psychological Monographs*, Vol. 80, No. 1 (1966), and Herbert M. Lefcourt, *Locus of Control* (New York: Wiley, 1976).

Some students react negatively to classes where the instructor encourages discussion and encourages students to develop their own views and answers. Their students protest, "I didn't pay good money to sit and listen to a bunch of uninformed people express their opinions. I can get that in any bar." This attitude is legitimate. It is also narrow-minded.

The Latin root for the word *education* means to 'draw out' not to 'shovel in.' A good education teaches you to think for yourself. It teaches you to ask good questions and then learn how to find the answers on your own. A good education does not give you a diploma for learning how to seek out an expert for any question you have. It teaches you how to both listen to authorities and come to your own conclusions.

The more you look to experts in a field of knowledge to tell you what to think, the more vulnerable you are to being misled by people who need to be admired as experts. The more that you find a workable balance between objective facts, your own knowledge, and good judgment, the more you will develop internally guided direction in your life.

"Internal" learners who have a clear sense of self-direction need and appreciate an instructor who will let them follow their own path. Such students get upset with instructors who tell them exactly what they must learn, in what way, and how they will demonstrate what they have learned. For them, a clearly defined course structure is abrasive. They feel handicapped more than helped. Such reactions are legitimate and narrow-minded.

In every field of study, certain basics must be mastered. There are basic terms and concepts that must be understood. There are some techniques that are fundamental to mastery of the subject even though the reasons may not be given, or, when given, don't make sense.

Curve Grading Versus Contracts

Viewing the instructor as an authority who tells you what to learn is usually linked to expecting the instructor to decide what grade you will receive. The traditional method of teaching usually implies using a class curve to determine student grades.

Grading "on the curve" means that all the scores are ranked from highest to lowest. Then the few highest scorers are given As. The next group, down to the midpoint in the class, receive Bs. Students whose scores fall below the class midpoint receive Cs. Any students with scores below a certain minimum level receive Ds and Fs.

Smart, hard-working, competitive students tend to like curve grading. Their As indicate that they are better than most other students. The problem with curve grading is that students who are not competitive may not even try. Curve grading increases competitiveness between students and decreases cooperation. Students are less likely to share notes, join together in study groups, or help each other because helping the other person may give that person a higher score and thus lower your grade. With curve grading, only a limited number of As and Bs are available.

Curve grading increases stresses and tensions when all the students in a certain class are good students. In such a class, anyone under the midpoint will get a C even though the same examination score in another class might be up in the B group.

To encourage good students to take courses where they might not do better than average, many colleges offered a new option. Some courses can be taken on a pass/no pass basis. With this option, a student can take a class which will broaden his or her education and earn credit for the course without a grade being assigned. Students taking pass/no pass courses can earn credit toward graduation requirements without risking lowering their grade point average (GPA).

To reduce competition and yet encourage good work, many instructors now teach their courses using a "contract" approach. The contract is that the instructor agrees at the beginning of the course to give you whatever grade you want to earn by doing a specific amount of work with a specific quality. You decide at the beginning what grade you want to receive in this class. Earning an A, B, or C is completely your choice.

The instructor has decided before the start of the course what activities and demonstrations of learning are worth an A, what you must do to earn a B, and what a C is worth. Then the instructor makes an agreement with you—that is, enters into a "contract" with you—guaranteeing that for doing the work you will get the grade you want.

This contract method may seem strange to you if you are expecting the old "grading on the curve" method. Some students are bewildered when they first encounter it. They are not used to the freedom and the responsibility. If you are not used to this approach, don't let it throw you. Once you get used to it, you'll probably like it better than the old way. With the contract approach, you will find that you don't have to compete with anyone except yourself. If you get a low grade, however, you are stuck with the knowledge that it was your own fault. You can't blame the other students for beating you out. You can't blame the instructor for being arbitrary or unclear.

The standards for A grades are usually high, but in the class working together to learn, there may be 50 to 70% of the class earning As. Who knows, with this sort of an opportunity you may do much better in school than you expect. You may become one of the many students who qualify for membership in Phi Beta Kappa, the national scholastic honorary society.

Three Basic Teaching Styles

STUDENT CENTERED

The contract method of determining grades is well suited to the instructor who makes students the focus of attention in the course. The instructor's main concern is your progress and development. Your personal growth is more important than the college, the instructor, the subject matter, or the discipline.

The instructor sees his or her primary responsibility as one of teaching students, not English, math, or chemistry. Such an instructor may be described as *altruistic*. The approach is one of selfless enjoyment in the experience of students gaining knowledge and understanding. Time outside the classroom is devoted more to grading class work and conferring with students than to doing the research and publishing that the college wants.

Several disadvantages to having an instructor who teaches in a student-centered fashion are:

You may have to do more work. The instructor wants papers, projects, and reports as a way of monitoring your progress.

You will be more than a face in the crowd. Your level of understanding, your study habits, and your ways of thinking may be seen for what they are. Some students can't handle that.

The instructor may make outrageous statements, challenge viewpoints, or take shocking positions in the service of getting you to think. This might not be a pleasant process if you dislike disagreement and conflict.

The instructor may give students little to imitate. Instead of giving students a model to follow or a clear way of thinking and acting that can be imitated, this instructor works at developing individuality. The goal is for everyone to discover their individual abilities and natures rather than to become like the instructor.

SUBJECT CENTERED

Some instructors make the subject matter of the course the main focus of attention. The more you share the instructor's awe, respect, and enthusiasm for the subject, the better you will do. With such an instructor, be prepared for an endless parade of glimpses at this field of study that he or she finds so absorbing.

In contrast to the student-centered approach, this instructor may be irritated with students who reject or challenge the views presented. Much preferred are brief sharings or insights and any supporting evidence you have found.

For some students, the instructor is a model to imitate. They adopt the instructor's vocabulary, clothing, and views.

Some disadvantages are:

In its extreme, the content-centered instructor is a sort of recruiter. He or she wants to draw students into a professional career in this field.

The instructor gains power over the student by becoming a coach on how to make it all the way through to the inside.

The student must adopt a certain viewpoint and vocabulary, which may reduce and limit self-development.

INSTRUCTOR CENTERED

Every campus has instructors who sparkle with charisma. They are exciting, inspired teachers. They can capture a room full of students and hold a class spellbound with extraordinary stories, histrionics, and impassioned appeals. They command attention. Their field of expertise is a medium, the classroom is their stage.

In such classes, your efforts to speak up or share your own experiences may not be well received. The charismatic instructor tends to be impatient when others become the center of attention. The purpose of the lecture hour is to inspire and motivate, not for students to discuss or share.

If you enjoy good performances and welcome inspirational lectures, you are well matched. If, on the other hand, you would rather have many pages of notes full of information at the end of the lecture, you may be disappointed.

Some disadvantages with charismatic instructor-centered classes are:

Your questions will be reacted to but not usually well answered because the instructor will be playing to the audience.

To be in the spotlight, the instructor may use the classroom as a forum to attack his or her profession and colleagues. Instead of learning about the value of the subject, you may learn what is wrong with it.

Although you are absorbed and captivated during lectures, you may realize later that you haven't learned many facts. You may find that most of your factual learning comes from the textbook and that the instructor gives the text little attention in class.

Reality

The best all-around teachers are usually some combination of all of the above. The more capable teachers enjoy having a room full of students eager to listen and learn. They enjoy being appreciated for their teaching skills. Good teachers like the subject and value their chosen field. They encourage student growth and make themselves available for conferences and discussions.

What do you do when a teacher is less than ideal? Do you get angry when you discover that you don't have a good match between yourself and the instructor?

What can you do if the instructor doesn't seem to know how to quiet several talkative students? Can you still learn something from an instructor whose religious or political views are contrary to yours? And what if you hear gossip that the instructor uses marijuana or has had an affair with a student?

By now we hope that you begin to realize, if you didn't know already, that finding a really good match between yourself and an instructor is not something that happens all the time. If one of your habits is to find something wrong with others, your instructors will give you plenty of opportunities. If you are an experienced "victim," then the college will provide you with many chances to be upset, complain to classmates, and attack instructors you've judged to be imperfect.

Action Project: Becoming A More Adaptable Learner

To help organize your efforts to benefit from this chapter, rate yourself on each of the styles listed below. Use numbers from 1 to 5 to indicate how much it is difficult (1) or easy (5) for you to function with each of the following styles.

____ Auditory   ____ Visual
____ Intellectual   ____ Metaphoric
     (Left-brained)   (Right-brained)
____ Friendly   ____ Distant
____ External   ____ Internal

After filling in your ratings for each style, look at the pairs of styles above and consider what you would have to do to shift from "either/or" ratings to "both/and." For example, if you gave a 4 to "Auditory" and a 1 to "Visual," ask yourself what steps you could take to do better in a class taught by a visually oriented instructor. You could, for example:

1. Find classmates who will tell you what they learned from the textbook readings.
2. Dictate the main points from the reading assignments and handouts onto cassette tape and then listen to the tapes.
3. Consciously work at improving your ability to acquire informa-

tion visually. For professional help, go to the reading improvement center.

If your ratings indicate that you are a good visual learner but find auditory learning more difficult, then some possible steps to take would be:

1. Take very good notes on what the instructor and your classmates say. After class fill in sentences and compare notes with other students.
2. Ask the instructor for suggested articles or books that cover the points you need to understand better.
3. Consciously work at listening and remembering what people say. *TIP:* Every so often, repeat back to the instructor what you believe has been said; for example, "Excuse me, I want to make sure I've accurately heard the main points. The main arguments in favor of the view are . . . ; is that correct?"

Organize your efforts in a way that works for you. A student who responded to our request for feedback told us:

I learned to type just before going to the university. I began to type my lecture notes each day, mainly as typing practice. I observed how much easier exam review was for me than for many of my residence friends. The typing was an automatic review of the day's ideas. I had a chance to fill in inadequate notes while I still remembered what had been said.

I am a more visual person than some. I find that making charts to compare and contrast differing views has been helpful. Similarities or differences can be highlighted with colored pencils.

Approach an imbalance between any of the pairs in a similar way. If you gave yourself a low rating on either the external or the internal of a pair, then consider challenging yourself to become *both* external *and* internal in how you function in courses.

Our experience is that the students who get the most out of school can discipline themselves to follow the tightly controlled steps used by some teachers. They can also create their own learning experiences when in a class taught by someone who gives few guidelines.

If you find yourself in a class where the instructor is overly controlling or overly permissive then:

Make an appointment to talk with the instructor. Be prepared to ask for what you want. Ask the permissive instructor for more structure if you need that. Ask the controlling instructor for freedom to do something different if you want that. You may be surprised at how easy it is to get what you want when you ask.

If asking doesn't work—or you don't want to ask—then try to adapt to your instructor's style. Instead of being angry at what the world has served up, see what you can learn from doing it the instructor's way. You may be surprised at what you discover.

In general, try to get as much out of every course regardless of who your instructor is or how much the teaching style does not fit your preferred learning style. Be open to try a new way of learning.

If you still have problems, go to the office or center that teaches studying and reading skills. The counselors there can be very helpful.

Learn how to be active in helping your instructors become better instructors.

Chapter 11

How To Influence Your Instructors

Do you know that students who track positives get more from their instructors than students who track negatives?

Do you know that many students are unaware of the effects of their behavior on instructors?

Do you know that you can increase your awareness of the effect you have on instructors by looking at ways to frustrate and irritate them?

Do you know that negative student behavior can lead to negative instructor behavior?

Do you know that you can get more from your instructors by complimenting them when they've done something you appreciate?

Helping Your Instructors Be Better Instructors

If you say to yourself, *"It's my job to help my instructors do well!"* you can have a profound effect on your instructors' performance. There are many things you can do as a student to make the lives of your instructors more pleasant and their performance more useful to you. Here is what students who get better teaching suggest.

Make Sure the Instructor Knows You

No matter how large the class, find some way to introduce yourself and let the instructor know why this course is important to you. Make an effort to let the instructor know you and recognize you. If you have special reasons for taking the course, let the instructor know what they are. Instructors always have choices about what material they cover or leave out, emphasize or skip over.

Reward Your Instructors for Good Teaching

When your instructors do something that you consider to be effective teaching, let your instructors know that you appreciate their teaching. Rewards for good teaching are few and far between. After a better than average lecture, tell your instructor what you liked about the lecture. Most students are reluctant to compliment their instructors. Most students don't want to appear to be apple polishers. Your instructors will probably be excellent judges of sincere comments and will appreciate what you have to say. Don't hold back your compliments. Let your instructors know you like their teaching.

How To Develop a Positive Action Plan

Do you know exactly what things instructors do that make them good instructors?

Can you clearly describe the specific, observable behaviors that you know are the basis for good teaching? Do you know what a student can do to reinforce and improve teaching quality?

Here are the basic steps to follow:

Step 1: TAKE A FEW MINUTES TO LIST ALL THOSE THINGS THAT GOOD TEACHERS DO. LIST SPECIFICS. LIST OBSERVABLE BEHAVIORS.

In the space below fill in a few specific, observable things that good teachers do, such as "Listens attentively when I ask a question." Saying that a teacher "is nice" is not an observable behavior. When you are through, get together with several other students and compare lists. Discuss the lists and revise them.

1. _____
2. _____
3. _____

4. _____
5. _____
6. _____
7. _____

Step 2: BRAINSTORM A LIST OF ALL THE REINFORCING THINGS YOU COULD DO IN RESPONSE TO A DESIRED TEACHING BEHAVIOR.

To brainstorm means to write out a list of ideas as fast as you can. The emphasis is on quantity, not quality. Be wild and imaginative. Be outrageous and funny. Do this with three or four other people and see how much fun brainstorming can be.

After about five minutes, stop and go through the list to see what things you could do. *NOTE:* You will continue to come up with ideas for the list for a few more hours, so wait a day or so before finishing your basic list.

1. _____
2. _____
3. _____
4. _____
5. _____
6. _____
7. _____
8. _____
9. _____

Step 3: TYPE OUT A COPY OF YOUR LISTS OF DESIRED TEACHING BEHAVIORS AND TEACHER REINFORCERS AND PLACE IT IN YOUR NOTEBOOK.

Step 4: NOW LOOK FOR THE FIRST POSSIBLE OPPORTUNITY TO OBSERVE A GOOD TEACHING BEHAVIOR AND REWARD IT!

Respond Positively to Good Instructional Behavior

When your instructors are doing things you consider to be good teaching, be very attentive. Nod; even smile. Instructors' actions are determined to a large extent by the attention they receive from students. When you and the other students indicate your approval of your instructors' good teaching behavior, you'll encourage your instructors to do more of the things you like and less of what you don't like.

If you don't see why your body language is important, imagine standing in front of a group of students who are nodding off to sleep, gazing out windows, carrying on private conversations, and generally acting disinterested. Would you be motivated to be enthusiastic and well prepared to teach this group of students?

If you have any doubt about the effect sincere attention and appreciation has on instructors, think about your own experiences. Think about the motivating effects that sincere attention has on you.

Provide Your Instructors with Feedback

If your instructors encourage periodic evaluations of their classroom performance, be sure to fill out their evaluations. Let your instructors know what you like! If you want to tell an instructor that there is something which needs to be improved, be sure to give an example of what you don't like and what you would like. There are few things worse than having a student tell you to improve some aspect of your teaching behavior but not be able to give you a clear example of what it is he or she would like you to do. Be sure you can give an example of what you would like to see more or less of (for example, clearer instructions and fewer personal stories).

Help Your Instructor Be Clear and Precise

Encourage your instructors to clearly define their expectations of students. If your instructor is unclear about an assignment, pleasantly ask him to restate the assignment. Don't hesitate to ask for clarification. If you didn't understand the assignment, more than likely other more timid students are sitting in class saying to themselves, "What is it he wants us to do?" You'll be doing yourself, your fellow students, and your instructor a favor by asking for clarification.

Regardless of how unclear an instructor may be, when you ask your clarifying question, don't make a big deal about how confused you are. Don't make your instructor look like an idiot. Just ask your instructor to clarify what he wants and thank him for his help.

If after asking for clarification regarding an assignment you are still confused, don't badger the instructor. Try not to say things like "I still don't know what you want!" or "You really haven't been clear as to the assignment!" More than likely you and several other students can figure out what your instructor is assigning. If not, step up after class and pleasantly point out your confusion. When you ask for clarification, ask confidently; try not to play the "bewildered idiot."

Unclear questions from instructors often turn students' stomachs. You're likely to think to yourself, "What the hell is it he's asking?" Don't let your gut reaction show! Pleasantly ask your instructor to restate his question. If your instructor's second attempt isn't any clearer than his first attempt, pleasantly indicate that you're unsure of the answer. Try to avoid throwing your hands into the air and saying, "I don't know what you're getting at!"

Prepare Good Questions Before Going to Class and
Always Try To Answer Your Instructors' Questions

As you read your assignments for class, decide what questions you would like your instructor to answer. In class, listen attentively to see if your instructor answers your questions. If not, don't be reluctant to pose your questions to your instructor.

Most instructors want students to ask good questions. Too often, students sit back timidly, afraid to ask questions. Instructors then go into a sweat, worrying whether the students have the least idea of what's going on.

Instructors prepare lectures hoping to stimulate students' inquisitiveness. If you sit back and fail to ask questions or turn your face to the floor every time an instructor poses a question, both you and the instructor will be losers. Give your instructors opportunities to demonstrate their intelligence. Ask good questions! Give yourself an opportunity to demonstrate your intelligence. Answer your instructors questions!

Attend All Classes

Instructors work hard to prepare lectures. When you decide to skip a class, you are saying to your instructors, "I don't believe what you are doing is of any value!" Show your instructors by your attendance that you value what they have to say. If you must miss a class, do not show up at the next session and ask, "Did I miss anything important?" Don't remind the instructor that you were absent. Just return to class and find out from a friend or another student what you missed.

Turn in Your Assignments on Time

Late assignments often suggest to your instructors that you lack enthusiasm for their courses. Some instructors reciprocate with a lack of enthusiasm for your procrastination by deducting points from late papers. Do your best to show you care. Don't say it with flowers! Say it with papers!

The Grand Scheme: Positive and Negative Effects

Students who get better teaching discover that POSITIVE STUDENT BEHAVIOR LEADS TO POSITIVE INSTRUCTOR BEHAVIOR.

Although our students have never claimed that reinforcing good teaching will turn an instructor from a Simon Legree into a Dale Carnegie, students who actively work to get better teaching are emphatic about the positive effect students can have on instructor performance.

What are the negative by-products of student behavior? Students who are aware of the effects students have on instructors are equally emphatic about the profound negative effect students can have on instructors' behavior.

Negative student behavior can lead to negative instructor behavior. Students are wonderful at describing ways to destroy the best of instructors. Some students gleefully describe stories relating how they spearheaded a well-planned attack on a high school teacher whom the students loathed. The sadistic glee of students is often shared by class members who remember a teacher from high school who found ill-prepared, unmotivated, and uncaring students too much to deal with.

Strangely enough, when college students somewhat shamefully list their adolescent behaviors, they often realize what a damaging effect their behavior may have had on that disliked high school instructor. Some high school teachers literally find the inconsiderate, unmotivated, and lackluster students not worth the effort. These unhappy instructors eventually resign themselves to collecting their paychecks and putting up with the daily task of teaching the "ungrateful."

The lot of the college instructor can sometimes be equally disheartening. College professors are known to complain of unmotivated, uncaring, and ill-prepared students. The cause of the professor's distress is often subtle and "hopefully" unconscious student behavior. In defense of themselves, college students often point out how unaware they are of the effect of their behavior on professors.

As is often the case, people are unaware of the effects of their behavior on others until it is too late. In your case, there has never been a better time to observe the behavior of college students which creates rather frustrated professors.

Notice Negative Effects on Your Instructors

As you go through the following list of "Behaviors Guaranteed To Frustrate Instructors," ask yourself:

> How often have I behaved this way to an instructor?
> What effect would this behavior have on me if I were the instructor?
> If I were the instructor, how would I respond to students who acted in such ways?

By taking the perspective of your instructor, you may get a better feeling for why it's academic suicide to get caught up in behaving inconsiderately toward your instructors. You may appreciate how easily professors can become disheartened by nice students who simply aren't aware of what it's like to deal with well-meaning but unthinking students.

Behaviors Guaranteed To Frustrate Instructors

ARGUE ANGRILY WITH INSTRUCTORS, ESPECIALLY OVER EXAMS

Students consistently describe instances in which frustrated classmates verbally attack instructors' statements. Sure, you have a right to your opinion. But, regardless of how seriously you differ with your instructor, you needn't argue. A huffy, heated attack on your instructor's position will gain neither of you anything but a mutual dislike for one another.

USEFUL ALTERNATIVE: Learn to present your difference of opinion assertively but without anger. Ask questions to find out why the differences exist. Turn the conflict into a learning experience.

TREAT CLASSES AS SOCIAL HOURS OR AS UNWANTED OBLIGATIONS

For a variety of reasons, students often carry on private conversations, act bored, show up late, sleep, leave class early, or simply play the fool in class. You wouldn't be paid for sleeping, playing cards, or socializing with your best friend if you were working a nursing shift or acting as foreman on an assembly line. Instructors are justified to feel that you don't belong in their courses if you appear to be disinterested in learning.

BE A KNOW-IT-ALL STUDENT

We've all experienced the know-it-all students who act as though no one has anything of importance to say but them. Know-it-alls are universally hated! Our students have heard comments to know-it-alls such as "Oh, we don't get to hear from you again, do we?" or "You're so smart! You always have the final word!"

USEFUL ALTERNATIVE: If you treat other students as valuable people from whom you can learn, you'll be way ahead of the game. Assume that everyone has something of value to say. Acknowledge other students' contributions. If you spend time trying to prove that your instructors and fellow students know less than you do, you can bet you'll come out on the short end of the stick.

TELL EMOTIONAL AND PERSONAL STORIES LEADING NOWHERE

Students often become so involved with class discussions that they go off into personal stories which are of no value to anyone. Instructors are just as guilty of overpersonalizing their courses. There are times when our personal experiences are relevant to the focus of class discussion. We simply urge you to always ask yourself, "Will the personal comment I'm going to make add to the class discussion, or do I just want to tell people about myself?"

Periodically, the focus of a class discussion can lead people to become heated, angry, elated, joyous, or just about any emotional state imaginable. When you become emotional in class, if you're like most people, you may have a tendency to allow your mouth to run off with your emotions. Students often define such emotional behavior as "spilling your guts." We've all spilled our guts at times. We're all human. But if you choose to avoid gut spilling, learn to ask yourself, "Do I really want to say what I am going to say when I feel like this? Do I want to think about what I am responding to and be sure that what I have to say is of value? If I do say something, need I be emotional?"

USEFUL ALTERNATIVE: Learning to think about what you're going to say and why you're going to say it is a skill everyone needs to practice. In your case, the crucial questions are "Will what I say be of value?" and "How can I say what I want so as to ensure it will be most useful to other people?"

EXPECT YOUR INSTRUCTORS TO BE OUTSTANDING EVERY DAY

All of us have days when we'd prefer to avoid contact with other people. Professors do not have the luxury of hiding in a closet until a bad mood passes. If they haven't had time to prepare for class, they still have to show up.

USEFUL ALTERNATIVE: Show a little compassion. Don't expect the impossible. No one can be outstanding daily. If your professor appears to be having an off day, work your hardest to do everything possible to make the class a good one. Be more attentive than ever. Ask good questions. Nod and smile at everything your instructor does well. (A word of caution: Don't overdo it. You needn't look like a smiling Cheshire cat. Just be positive.)

After class, if you liked your instructor's performance, go out of your way to let him know he did well. It's doubly important on tough days for instructors to know that they can ride out a storm.

TELL OTHER STUDENTS WHAT YOU DISLIKE ABOUT THE
INSTRUCTOR—NEVER GO DIRECTLY TO THE INSTRUCTOR

It is easy for you to complain to other students about a particular instructor. The problem is that your complaints won't help your instructor teach better or your classmates learn more. Your complaints may result in students responding negatively toward your instructor, which will surely hurt his performance. So why make things tough for your instructor, your fellow students, and yourself?

USEFUL ALTERNATIVE: Encourage other students to get the most out of your instructors' courses. Never downgrade your instructors to other students. Try to help your instructors, not hurt them! Encourage yourself and other students to look for the good points in your instructors. As we've stated throughout this chapter, try to create a climate in which your instructors can do an even better job.

If you decide that you just don't have the time or interest to help your instructors improve their performance, at least keep your negative comments to yourself. Don't make other students suffer who are willing to try to help your instructors.

BE IRRITATING TO AN INSTRUCTOR WHO IRRITATES YOU

Don't cut class, drop the course, or transfer to another class when you have a rotten instructor. Attend class and do things that communicate your negative opinion.

Take a paperback book to class and read it while the instructor lectures.

If you knit, take your knitting to class and work on it instead of taking notes. Click the needles loudly if you can.

Sit back with your arms crossed and refuse to take any notes while everyone else is writing furiously. Scowl and sneer at those who are taking notes.

Just as the instructor leads up to an important point in the lecture, lean over and whisper loudly to a classmate. Include muffled laughs and snickers. Keep it up, pretending not to notice how distracting your whispering is to the class and how angry the teacher is getting.

USEFUL ALTERNATIVE: Be responsible for your feelings. When you blame others for your feelings you are letting other people control you. Consider what is happening as information about yourself and try to learn a lesson.

TALK DOWN TO INSTRUCTORS YOU THINK ARE "LOSERS"

If you have six or seven instructors, you will probably feel that one of them is excellent, most of the others are adequate and that one is a loser. Here is a great opportunity to sneer at, be sarcastic with, and show open contempt for a teacher. You can prove to other students that you are so tough and "with it" that you can put down instructors to their faces.

USEFUL ALTERNATIVE: If you can't avoid being sarcastic, then consider not saying anything at all. It is tough enough being an instructor, especially when you know that some of the students openly dislike you. Instructors have all the fears that you might have if you had to make useful presentations to the same group day after day.

Remember too that it is a function of your human nature to like one of your instructors the best and another the least. If you really wanted better teaching, you could give the instructor a sincere compliment after a better than average lecture. You could do the various things that we recommend at the beginning of this chapter to enforce good teaching. If you are critical of teachers in a way that is not helpful or useful to them, you need to have a target for your disgust more than you need good teaching, so don't take yourself too seriously!

ASK YOUR INSTRUCTORS TO BE PERSONAL COUNSELORS

It's natural for you to want to be friendly with your instructors. That's great! Unfortunately, some students expect too much of them. These students expect their instructors to be terribly interested in all of their personal ideas, interests, and problems. Most instructors want to be friendly with their students but are not in a position to be all things to all students.

The difficulties begin to arise when students start dropping in all the time to talk, unload their personal problems, and generally cut into the rather tight schedules that many professors work within. Professors often feel uncomfortable discouraging drop-ins. Few professors want to be known as uncaring or uninterested in their students. Professors want the best for their students and are usually willing to try to help. It's simply unfair to ask professors to spend their time socializing on the job or solving your personal problems.

USEFUL ALTERNATIVE: Try not to ask your instructors to do more than they are professionally equipped to handle. If you need help with personal problems, see the professional counselors at your college or talk to your best friends.

DEMAND THAT YOUR INSTRUCTORS GIVE YOU SPECIAL FAVORS AND CONSIDERATION

If you think we're making a big deal out of nothing, let that thought pass. We've known students who will miss half of the semester, come in, and ask if they can't somehow get the information from the instructor. We've known students who would ask instructors if they could take the midterm two weeks late because they were leaving early on spring break for a vacation in Florida. Our favorite is the student who called an instructor at 8:00 a.m. on Saturday to find out if he missed anything important during the week of classes he missed.

USEFUL ALTERNATIVE: Most of your instructors will be people who are interested in your academic and personal well-being. Instructors understand that you may run into financial, transportation, health, and numerous problems which interfere with successful performance in class. Don't be afraid to let your instructor know when an event drastically alters your performance. If you're ill with the flu for two weeks, let your instructor know why you're missing class. Instructors appreciate knowing why students aren't coming to class.

Minor problems should be kept to yourself. If your car breaks down and you miss class, don't come in with a big song and dance expecting your instructor to pray for your car. Accept the bad with the good. Borrow notes from someone in the course. Don't expect your instructor to repeat an entire lecture for you.

In short, if something of tremendous importance necessitates your needing to ask a favor from your instructor, DON'T HOLD BACK!!!! If minor irritations of life have made your student life a bit miserable, assume you'll recover. Don't throw your personal problems at your instructor. What you'll probably find is that you'll live happily ever after.

"How Can I Turn a Bad Situation Around?"

Avoid Flunking Courses by Being Diplomatic and Willing To Work

If you are likely to receive a D or an F in a course, you can often salvage a bad grade. But you have to learn to be diplomatic and pleasant to deal with.

Too often, students having academic problems approach instructors with unbelievable stories, rather than accepting that a straightforward approach is best.

Go talk to your instructor and ask for a chance to make up your work. *Go with a plan!* Offer to make up exams. Ask if you can write an extra paper or rewrite the project you threw together the night before it was due. Explain why you are willing to. Instructors are much more willing to give students a chance to make amends if the students act like adults and are willing to admit that they have done poorly and are willing to turn over a new leaf rather quickly.

Most instructors will give you a chance. Bad grades are not permanent unless you allow them to be.

For example, if you do poorly on the midterm or final, ask to take the make-up exam. Ask for a chance to show that you do know the material. (Maybe you didn't then but things have changed now.) Even if the instructor says you can't take the test to change your grade, ask to take it anyway to see for yourself if you can do better. Assuming that you will get a better score, this will have a psychological effect on the instructor later.

If you anticipate a bad grade in a course because you haven't been able to get all of the work in, but you want to earn a good grade, then consider asking the instructor to submit an "incomplete" on the grade sheet. Your instructor may be willing to follow school policies that allow students to complete course work after the course is over. At most schools you have at least a semester.

You can change the past if you want to. A sincere request for another chance, a specific plan about what you will do, and a commitment to do it will influence the hardest of instructors and deans.

Whatever you do, don't just quit. If your college courses are too difficult to handle, you don't have to become a "dropout." Don't just disappear or not show up for registration. Go talk to your advisors and explore the possibility of "stopping out." The advisor can arrange for you to take a leave of absence and help arrange for you to come back later.

Instructors Are Human Beings

The list of "Behaviors Guaranteed To Frustrate Instructors" is not meant to convey the message that instructors are special people who have to be treated with kid gloves. Absolutely not! Instructors are human beings who react to pressures, demands, problems, stresses, and all the other factors that complicate our lives.

Instructors are human beings just like you. They prefer to be treated nicely. They want you to come to their classes and learn every good thing you ever wanted to know. Most instructors will work overtime to help you. If you'll look for the good in your instructors and try to make their classes pleasant and enlightening, most of them will do everything humanly possible to make your life as a student a good life.

But remember, if you ask too much of your instructors, cut into their personal lives, appear disinterested in their courses, or generally make a pest of yourself, you'll encourage your professors to be sullen and angry individuals. You'll hear instructors complain about not having enough time to get their work done. You'll hear professors gripe about students who don't show up in class, don't ask good questions, don't seem to be interested in learning, and all in all are no joy to teach.

What we're suggesting to you is the simple fact that *You make a difference! You can either choose to help your instructors be better instructors who enjoy teaching or choose to behave in ways that cause instructors to be unhelpful and boring. Instructors who go around with a chip on their shoulders are often created by students who don't appear to care about their education.* The choice is yours. We suspect you'll want to do your best to help your instructors do their best possible for you and your fellow students.

Last but not least, accept the fact that you will have great instructors, mediocre instructors, and some who appear to be like Darth Vader. Regardless, follow the suggestions we've made. Try to help every instructor be a good instructor. It's all up to you!

Action Project: Turn Your Negatives into Positives

1. ___ ___ ___ What behaviors or habits do you exhibit in a class that you don't particularly care for, which might result in your instructor developing a negative attitude toward you?

2. ___ ___ ___ What could you be doing instead to draw more positive reactions toward you? List the behaviors.

3. ___ ___ ___ Practice your new behaviors for a month. Then come back to this space and describe how your behavior

has changed in the class. Discuss whether or not by behaving differently, you have developed a different attitude toward the class and the instructor.

4. ___ ___ ___ If your behavior in a class changed, did your perception of the class change? What does this tell you about the effects of your habits on your attitudes?

Action Review for Getting Better Teaching

1. _____ Take some time with several classmates to develop a list of things that good teachers do. List specific, observable behaviors.

2. _____ List all those things you might do that could be rewarding for an instructor.

3. _____ Observe each instructor to see how much or how little the desired teaching behaviors occur.

4. _____ Compliment and reward instructors who do many of the things you list as good teaching. Be specific. Let instructors know what you appreciate. *Remember:* The more quickly you reward a desired behavior, the more effective your reward.

5. _____ List all the things that students do that can irritate, bother, and upset instructors and make teaching an unpleasant experience.

6. _____ Observe how you react when a teacher is less than what you would like. Ask yourself, "Do I do any of the things which upset and frustrate teachers?"

7. _____ Track positives. When an instructor is low in giving you good teaching behaviors, look for any little signs of improvement and immediately reinforce the improvement.

8. _____ Ask yourself, "Am I a rewarding person to have in class?" If you aren't, then here is a good chance to practice. *Remember:* Trite as it is, there is a lot of wisdom in the old idea of "An apple for the teacher!"

Chapter 12

How To Have a Few Good Friends and Gain Support from Your Family

Did you know that loneliness is a problem for many college students?

Did you know that frequency of contact is an important factor in the development of feelings of friendship?

Did you know that it is possible to increase the number of friends that you have?

Would you know what to do if you felt unworthy of friendship?

Did you know that it is possible for a college student to create a plan for gaining more support from family members and to succeed with it?

"Dr. James?"

"Hello, Sid, come on in."

"Dr. James, could I ask you a question?"

"Sure, Sid. What is it?"

"In psychology class you teach us a lot about how to understand human behavior. But I can't find the answer to my question anyplace."

"What's that?"

"How do you keep from being so lonely?"

"Well, what have you tried?"

"I used to drive people places in my car—sort of a free taxi service—but that didn't work. I was moving and hauling stuff all over the place, but still no one was friends with me."

"What else have you tried?"

"For a while I paid for everything. Cokes, hamburgers, movie tickets, popcorn, ice cream, but that kept me broke. Then I tried telling jokes. I bought a joke book and each time I was going to be with people I would memorize four or five jokes to tell."

"How did that work?"

"People laughed sometimes, but I couldn't always tell if they were laughing at me or the joke. It didn't make anyone more friendly. It always ends up the same: They thank me for the ride or the ice cream, or laugh at the joke, and then go out with other people. I need friends too! How can I get people to like me?"

The Loneliness Problem

College counselors and advisors know that loneliness is a major problem for many college students. It is hard to be enthusiastic about studying and learning when you feel homesick and lonely.

The reason the loneliness problem has such a negative impact on students and affects their grades can be understood by looking at the hierarchy of needs described by Abraham Maslow (see page 150). The need to be accepted and liked by others is a stronger need than needs for personal growth and knowledge. When the need to be accepted and liked dominates a student's thoughts and concerns, little energy is available for studying and learning. Maslow's description of the hierarchy of needs helps explain why it is so hard to study when you feel that no one likes you or loves you and why it is hard to read in the library while rehearsing an imaginary conversation with someone sitting nearby.

A view which is developing about the great popularity of cults is that the cults take care of the need for friendship and acceptance. For a person who is lonely, the invitation to join into a group and be a warmly welcomed friend is enticing. Some cult leaders instruct members to work the streets near counseling centers looking for lonely students.

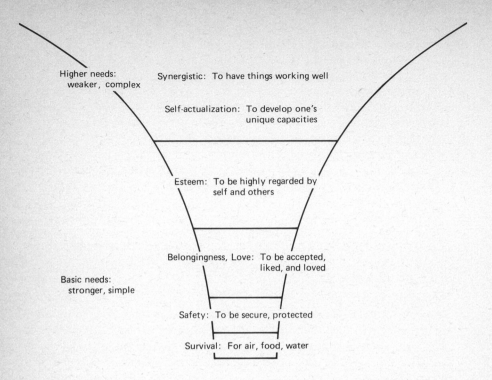

Higher needs:
weaker, complex

Synergistic: To have things working well

Self-actualization: To develop one's
unique capacities

Esteem: To be highly regarded by
self and others

Belongingness, Love: To be accepted,
liked, and loved

Basic needs:
stronger, simple

Safety: To be secure, protected

Survival: For air, food, water

Most cults involve so much of a person's total time, however, that not much is left available for pursuing a college career. There are many things you can do to increase the number of friends you have and the amount of warm support you get from your family. It is not necessary to struggle through school with a rather lonely existence, hoping that things will get better later on.

As with success in school, you have choices about how many friends you have. Having friends is not a matter of luck or having money or having a great personality. Feelings of friendship develop between people as a result of a combination of variables that you can influence.

Have Frequent Contact

Research into the sources of feelings of friendship shows that the main contributing factor is frequency of contact. That is partly why we have emphasized so often in this book that a realistic plan for being more successful in school should include frequent opportunities to spend time with friends.

Research in college dorms, in housing projects, and in neighborhoods shows a consistent relationship between feelings of friendship and how often people have contact with each other. One study of married students in campus housing, for example, showed that couples living in certain apartments developed friendships more frequently than would be predicted by chance. These people were living in apartments at the foot of the stairs. Observation finally revealed that the couples were seen more frequently because the garbage cans were located near the bottom of the stairs!

Many such studies show that, in general, the closer you live to someone, the more likely it is that he or she will remain a close friend. Once you understand how frequency of contact influences feelings of friendship, you can see why certain conditions predict that some students will have fewer friends at school. Don't take a lack of friends personally if any of the following apply to you:

Living at home instead of in student housing.
Not joining a fraternity or sorority.
Being married to someone who is not a student.
Working full time while going to school.
Studying all the time.
Training full time for individual athletic events such as swimming or long-distance running.
Being a quiet loner who rarely talks to anyone.

To have more frequent contact with other students, get involved in one or more of the many extracurricular activities on campus. These include:

volunteering to serve on committees for student body activities, such as Homecoming or Parents Weekend or producing the yearbook.
intramural sports.
social action groups, such as Greenpeace, environmentalists, or those that provide food for the needy.
special-interest clubs and groups such as the psychology club, ski club, foreign students, or photography club.
the school newspaper.
church-sponsored social centers near campus.

There is a wide variety of activities available to you that will bring you into contact with other students with similar interests. Keep in mind that it is not unusual for a beginning student to feel lonely. Loneliness is a normal experience when in a totally new situation without contact with old friends and family.

If you feel homesick, then phone home, write, or exchange cassette-tape letters with your family. Get a cassette tape recorder and make a short tape to send home. Your family would like to hear from you. Sending tapes from time to time will also help them make the transition with you as you assume your new role as an educated adult.

Obtain the addresses of several good friends from high school and write or send cassette tapes to them. Exchanging tapes will probably be better than writing because you gain much more from hearing a familiar person talking. Besides, people will often say things on tape about personal experiences that they wouldn't want to put into writing!

Go to the Counseling Center

All college students, at one time or another, have periods of feeling lonely and depressed. When this happens to you, remember that such feelings are part of being human. Regardless of how special or unique you believe your loneliness or depression is, the school employs counselors who can probably be very helpful. They won't have a miracle pill for you to get rid of unpleasant feelings; they'll have something much better. They will show you how to get through the unpleasant period while the natural emotional processes of self-healing are operating.

Even if you are reluctant to see a counselor, telephone or drop by the counseling center anyway. You can always try other solutions if you don't like the counselor. In fact, you may not want to talk with a counselor at all, preferring to use other center resources. Many counseling centers have libraries of useful books and cassette tapes on how to deal with depression, get over nervousness, be less shy, and so forth.

Emotional upsets are a normal part of college life. You don't have to try to handle them by yourself. It is not a sign of strength to mask your feelings with drugs or put on a front of happiness. Emotional strength develops from feeling whatever you feel and letting another human being be close to you when things aren't working perfectly.

Let People Know You

If you want people to accept you and like you, then you have to let them know what you feel, think, and do. If people have very little experience of you as a person, there is very little for them to relate to. Accept the fact that when some people learn about your feelings and thinking, they won't like what they hear. That's okay. No matter what you are like as a person, someone is going to dislike how you are. That is the way the world works. Trying to avoid being disliked will prevent you from being liked. Allowing people to know more about you is the only way to gain the friendships and acceptance that you need.

Be a Good Listener

People you have contact with will feel friendlier if you have a sincere personal interest in them and if they discover that you have attitudes and interests similar to theirs.

How do you accomplish this? Ask questions and listen with an open mind.

Dale Carnegie, author of *How To Win Friends and Influence People*, states, "You can make more friends in two months by being interested in other people than you can in two years by trying to get other people interested in you." Why should other people be interested in you if you aren't interested in them?

So, do not work at being liked. Work more at finding out what is likeable about each person you have contact with.

Accepting Versus Judging

Good listeners have a wide range of acceptance for what they learn about others. This is why so many people feel friendly toward a person who is accepting and tolerant. If we compare observing, open-minded people with those who are more judgmental in their reactions, the ranges of acceptance and rejection look like the following:

Open-minded

accept	neutral	reject

Judgmental

accept	neutral	reject

Notice that the open-minded person not only has a wider range of acceptance but also a wider neutral range. This means that much of what is learned is neither accepted nor rejected.

A judgmental person, even though remaining silent, eventually communicates through facial expressions, body language, and other reactions the attitude of "no one should think that" or "that's sick."

If the person you are listening to has attitudes and opinions that you dislike, then the chances are low that you will be a good friend of that person. You can have empathy for the individual, but you probably will not have much in the way of friendship.

A quick way to become more open-minded about other people and less judgmental is to develop the habit of mentally responding "that's okay" when you learn about another person's thoughts or attitudes.

Frequency of contact with others will make very little difference and will not lead to close feelings of friendship if you constantly have a judgmental attitude about the way other people think and live their lives.

Guidelines for Developing Friendships

So let's say that you are more open to doing things with people, to increasing the amount of contact that you have, and that you are becoming less judgmental by saying to yourself fairly frequently, "that's okay." After you've done these several things, here then are some guidelines to follow that will help promote a developing friendship.

Let people know you. Ask people to do things with you. Take some risks. Allow yourself to reveal personal thoughts, feelings, wishes, and interests even though you run the risk of rejection.

Develop a curiosity about other humans. Ask questions and find out what is important to others.

Don't start off by trying to flatter or praise the person. Too much praise has the reverse effect. People become suspicious. They are put on guard, wondering if you're trying to sell something or if you might be after something.

Avoid giving lots of praise to everyone. Praise from a person who thinks that everyone is fantastic all the time is not valued as much as a compliment from someone who gives occasional praise when it is deserved.

Wait until a person knows that you have seen something worthy of interest or praise before making a comment. Your praise will then be experienced as deserved, rather than as manipulated.

Express some disagreement if you in fact disagree with another person's viewpoint. In good friendships, people can honestly and spontaneously react with a negative comment or feelings of dislike and know that the friendship will not be lost.

Aim at having fun with people. Don't work at being liked. Find things to laugh about, and this includes yourself. Don't take yourself too seriously. Remember, the shortest distance between two people is laughter.

Indicators of Friendship

The steps and guidelines outlined above are only able to lay the groundwork for a good beginning. Once you are doing the above, more subtle factors come into play. Here are some features of good friendships:

Friends feel equal to each other. Feelings of friendship cannot exist when you feel superior or inferior to someone.

Friends are comfortable being seen together, letting people know they are friends.

Friends reveal private thoughts and feelings to each other. They share personal feelings and private thoughts not usually revealed to others. Their openness with each other is natural and spontaneous. They laugh together.

Friends can be trusted with confidential information. One of the fastest ways to destroy a friendship is to tell other people about something that you've been told in confidence.

Friends accept each other as they are. If you have a close friend, you allow that person to see you as you really are. You do not contrive or attempt to manipulate that person's perceptions of you to get that person to think of you in a certain way.

Friends experience each other as unique. A friend says that no person on earth is quite like his or her close friend.

Friends have the freedom to disagree with each other. Friends can become irritated or angry if that's how they truly feel. You don't feel truly close to someone who is never angry at you. In any relationship the strong positive feelings tend to disappear if negative ones are controlled and suppressed.

Friends are not jealous of each one having other friends. A good friendship is freeing, not limiting or controlling.

Feel Worthy of Friendship

The problem of not having many friends may not be from a lack of knowledge about what to do. Neither is it usually from not making an effort to be friendly. In some cases, the problem stems directly from the fact that an individual does not feel worthy of having friends.

Do you feel worthy of having good friends? How do you react to the person who says, "Hi! Let's go to a movie together"? How do you react to the person who walks up and starts talking with you and wants to continue talking for thirty minutes or an hour? Do you get nervous and find some excuse to get away? Do you have a negative opinion of anyone who would want to be friends with you?

If you find yourself uncomfortable when people make efforts to be friends with you, then take a little time to sit down with a pad of paper and fill out as long a list as you can in answer to these questions: What are all of the good reasons people would enjoy being friends with me? In what ways am I a nice person to be around? What are all the things I like and appreciate about myself?

If you find yourself feeling uncomfortable about attempting to answer such questions, then you may have been raised to avoid feelings of self-esteem. Conscious self-esteem is necessary, however, for any person to function well in the world. Self-esteem acts as an insulating buffer against unfounded criticisms. Self-esteem allows you to accept people's praise and affections as legitimate. It is not conceited to think well of yourself. Conceit means to feel superior to others and inform them about it. Self-esteem means to feel basically good about yourself even though you still have a lot to learn.

Be Assertive

If you sit back and passively hope that people will go out of their way to work at being friends with you or to give you praise and recognition, you are likely to be disappointed. As with other aspects of your

155

life, once you decide to take some initiative and to make a reasonable effort to get yourself what you would like to have, you will find that your life goes much better. One of the important lessons of life seems to be to learn how to develop friendships, how to be a good friend, and how to gain the support of other people. It could be that learning how to develop and maintain friendships and gain support will prove to be one of the most valuable abilities you learn in college.

If you feel that you lack assertiveness, we recommend reading several books on becoming more assertive. They will provide excellent advice and examples on how to behave in ways that will help you improve your interaction skills.

If gaining support from others is important to you, we think the following story will show how you can influence other people to change how they treat you by changing how you interact with them. As you'll see, the principles described in Chapter 11, "How To Influence Your Instructors," were used by a student to gain more attention and friendship from her father.

Barbara's Story

Barbara was starting her sophomore year in nursing school when she took introductory psychology. As a course assignment she was required to do a "behavior-change project." The project involved using principles of behavioral change with a person she had frequent contact with in daily life.

Other students in the class went to work on younger sisters, neighbor children, bus drivers, talkative roommates, boyfriends who drove too fast, smokers, overweight friends, and other available subjects. Barbara decided to use her father as the subject for her project.

Barbara lived at home and her relationship with her father was very poor. She said,

> We were always looking for ways to cut each other. He enjoyed saying rotten things about nurses to me. If he'd say, "good morning" to me, I'd say, "what's good about it!" If I came home from school excited about something and wanted to talk about it, he would just sit there in his chair and keep on reading. He didn't care about anything that was happening to me. Once when I was trying to talk to him about school he got up and walked out of the room. Didn't say a word. Just walked out.
>
> He is retired, so he is usually home during the day. I know he likes it if when I'm home at lunch time, I make a bowl of soup for him. I'd go into the kitchen and make myself something. He would get his hopes up and then be disappointed when he saw I only fixed something for myself. Chocolate cake is his favorite, so when I baked something I made sure it was *not* chocolate cake.
>
> When we were assigned the project, I decided to see if I could improve my life at home. It is hard enough getting through nursing school without al-

156

ways having a big hassle at home. I've been dreaming about going into nursing for a long time. It's exciting! I wanted my family to care!

Barbara's Plan for Herself

Barbara decided that each time her father responded pleasantly or positively she would be pleasant to him and do something special to show her appreciation for his interest in her. The slightest positive gesture from him would be immediately attended to by her. She would try never to overlook the slightest improvement, no matter how small or weak. Her goal was to increase the number of times her father showed interest in her and the depth of his interest.

Following the procedure recommended in class, Barbara outlined these steps:

Desired project goal: Father to greet me cheerfully each morning; show interest in what is happening at school; talk with me about school.

Current level of desired behavior: Seldom looks at me or listens when I am talking about school; never asks about school.

Reinforcements to father for increase in desired behavior: Bowl of soup at lunch; bake cookies and chocolate cake; smile and say "Thanks for talking with me"; kiss on the cheek.

Three weeks later Barbara reported the results of her project to the class:

My first chance to use a reinforcement was during a lunch time. I talked with Dad for several minutes, and he listened without looking at his magazine. I didn't try to push my luck by going on too long, so I got up and asked him if he would like for me to fix him a bowl of soup. His face brightened up. He smiled and said, "Yes."

In the morning if he said "hello" to me, I'd smile and say "hello" and kiss him on the cheek. Mornings are much more pleasant now.

After about three times fixing him soup at lunch, he began showing more interest and would ask questions. Then one evening he asked me to tell him about a book I read, and we spent almost twenty minutes talking. I immediately got up and went out to the kitchen and baked him a batch of cookies.

Last Friday afternoon I got home about 1:30. He got up from his chair as soon as he heard me come in and came over and said: "I've been waiting for you. I would like to know more about what you are doing in school if you have time to talk." Did I ever! We spent *two hours* talking. That is the longest my father has had a conversation with me in my whole life! It was great! He was *really* interested. When we finished I gave him a big hug, said how great it was talking with him, and went out and baked him a chocolate cake.

(Barbara suddenly grew quiet. Her eyes started to water, and she struggled to hold back tears. Her voice choked up a little as she went on.) Something happened this morning that isn't in my written report. I was getting ready to leave for school and Dad came up and put his arms around me. He said, "Barbara, I want to take you out to dinner next week. I want to get to know you better before it's too late."

Like many people who want their lives to be better, Barbara decided to be more responsible for how well things were going at home. She took steps to improve how she and her father got along.

A self-motivated person, who is willing to try something different and open to changing certain habits, learns how to manage the activity of learning. Knowing how to modify your behavior on your own by learning directly from life's experience is an essential skill to develop because there will always be problems and challenges in your life that no one prepared you for and that no one can teach you how to handle well. You have to learn some things all by yourself—and that is the focus of the next chapter.

Action Project for Gaining More Support from Your Family

Most students want and appreciate support from their families. Yet students often report that they receive less praise and recognition for their academic accomplishments than they hoped for. In fact, it is not uncommon for a family member to be critical or to make discouraging remarks about academic pursuits.

If you have an upsetting conflict with a family member and would like to make things more pleasant, review "Barbara's Plan for Herself." Then develop a plan of action that has a realistic chance of leading to an improvement.

To improve your contact with your family, however, you may also have to engage in some uncomfortable self-examination. Can you admit to yourself that you have been acting in ways that maintain the conflict?

If there are no big problems with your family members except lack of interest and support, then develop a plan of action for yourself based on the principles described in this chapter. Think about how you would like things to be between yourself and your family, and then take the necessary steps.

Action Project for Developing More Friends

Review the chapter, outlining the principles related to creating friendships. Then select someone to test the principles on. Choose a person that you feel equal to, someone likely to have attitudes and interests similar to yours. To increase your chance of success, select a person who is easily available to you. Then you'll have more opportunities to have frequent contact.

Start by having frequent but brief contacts with the person. Develop the habit of saying "Hi!" as you walk by. Wave to the person as you pass. Nod and smile whenever you have an opportunity. Find out the person's name and say hello, using this person's name, every time you have a chance.

As you sense feelings of friendly recognition developing, be ready for an opportunity to ask the person one or two questions about himself or herself. Be specific. Ask, "How are your examinations going this term?" or "What do you think of the President's announcement yesterday?"

Be willing to reveal your private attitudes or feelings briefly and then quickly focus attention back onto the other person. Don't be overly quick to like a person; don't be too eager, not at first.

Be a good listener. Listen with interest and an open mind. Try to learn what it is like to be the other person. Try to discover what is unique about this individual. Then, as you find out what he or she is really like, let yourself warm up more.

Don't be overly concerned if at first you feel that you are manipulating or doing what is so obvious that the person will see through it. People will be flattered that you are making the effort. What you're

159

doing is acting as people do who have good friends. When you conduct yourself in a new way, at first you are very aware of it. But as you practice, and see that it works, then it gradually becomes a habit. You become unaware of what you're doing, and it becomes more natural for you. Your goal is to concentrate less on having friends and to focus more on being a good friend to others.

REMEMBER: The best way to have good friends is to be one!

Suggested Readings

Bry, Adelaide. *Friendship: How To Have a Friend and Be a Friend* (New York: Grosset & Dunlap, 1979).

Emery, Stuart. *Actualizations: You Don't Have To Rehearse To Be Yourself* (Garden City, N.Y.: Doubleday, Dolphin, 1978).

Hearn, Janice. *Making Friends, Keeping Friends* (Garden City, N.Y.: Doubleday, 1979).

Shedd, Charlie. ed. *You Are Somebody Special* (New York: McGraw-Hill, 1978).

Chapter 13

Learning What No One Can Teach You

Do you know that "commencement" means beginning?

Do you learn useful lessons from your everyday experiences?

Do you know that self-actualization is a predictable need?

Do you agree with Socrates that it is important to know yourself?

Have you noticed that some people gain strength from adversity?

Could you list the qualities and traits of people with survivor personalities?

Did you know that a talent for serendipity can be learned?

Going Beyond Your Teachers

Educators call graduation "commencement." Why? They want to remind graduates that the end of formal schooling is not the end of education. For the person who is a constant learner, life is a never-ending school. Everyday experiences offer many rich and valuable lessons. One of the main purposes of a good education is to teach you good learning habits and how to manage your own continuing development. Good teachers will show you how to go beyond their teaching. The real excitement in learning comes when you move past the level where others can tell you what you should learn or know. Much of the excitement of being fully alive as an adult is to recapture some of the wonderful curiosity that you used to feel as a child.

You use good judgment, of course. You're not going to give your curiosity such free rein that you harm people or do things that would cause serious damage. But it's the sort of curiosity that allows you to ask a question with sincere interest, even if it might possibly embarrass you. You experiment with something and do it in a way so that if anything goes wrong, you will be the only person hurt.

People who explore, grow, and develop are people who take risks. When people try to avoid looking bad or giving a poor impression, they don't learn much. Self-directed learning increases as you develop self-confidence and begin to sense that what is best for you is not always approved by others.

Arranging for Self-Actualization

Abraham Maslow spent many years studying people he described as "self-actualizing." As pictured on page 150, he concluded that self-actualization emerges after the more basic needs are under reasonable control. According to the hierarchy of needs, energy for learning and developing emerges automatically after you've taken care of survival, safety, friendship, and esteem needs.

How well are you doing? Are you arranging for self-actualization by taking care of other important needs?

Assessment of Needs

For each of the areas below, first rate yourself as you see things now, using this rating scale:

1. Very concerned about this. This is a problem area for me.
2. Needs improvement.
3. Reasonably satisfied, but could be better.
4. Everything satisfactory.
5. In excellent shape here. Am very pleased.

Second, write a statement in the space provided about how you would like to have things a year from now.

Survival: Have good physical health; good eating habits; income is enough to pay bills and rent; have time for enjoying myself.

Safety and Security: Feel secure in job, in residence, in family and community; have some reserves and assets to fall back on in an emergency. People feel safe around me. I don't attack or threaten others.

Acceptance and Belonging: People like me and love me. I'm close to relatives, family, and friends; get along with most neighbors; am a welcome member at church, school, and in other places. I welcome others as friends.

Esteem: I do things that make me feel good about myself. I like myself. Most people like me and respect me. I learn from mistakes; I'm open to unpleasant information and appreciate constructive criticism. I appreciate other's accomplishments.

Self-Actualization: I ask lots of questions, seek new experiences, and take risks. I enjoy self-improvement. I act according to my emotional reading of situations and by logic and reason. Every year of my life is different from the last. I'm very curious. I'm discovering my unique nature. I experience most others as unique.

Third, consciously decide to improve several areas in which you would like things to be better. Develop a realistic plan of action for yourself. Ask, "What specific steps could I take to gradually take care of this need better?"

Developing a Survivor Personality

Self-actualizing people survive better than people whose main concerns are safety and security. People whose fear of risk and loss prevent them from taking new actions or having new experiences don't survive well. They are easily threatened. They are afraid they may look foolish. They clutch up when worried about what others may think. They flounder when dealing with the unknown.

People who handle life best have a knack for turning difficulties into growth experiences. They keep positive attitudes in negative situations. This is why viewing life as a school is practical and useful. *When trouble develops* you survive difficulty more capably when you focus in the growth direction. Perhaps you've noticed how much we've demonstrated growth reactions throughout the book. In the opening chapter, we emphasized being responsible for yourself. In the chapter on working with instructors, we suggested using difficulties with your instructor as a way to learn to handle people better. Throughout the book, whenever any difficult situation develops, our approach has been to show you how you can handle the difficulty in a way that makes you a stronger, more capable person.

Gaining Strength from Adversity

There is an old saying that "Good mariners are not created by calm seas." In fact, the purposes of the Outward Bound program trace back to the observation that when ships sink at sea, the old-timers are more likely to survive the hardship than younger, stronger people.

During the Depression in the 1930s a few people went against the tide and refused to be swept away by mass despair. Even though thousands were destitute, some people found ways to be happy and enjoy being alive. Using their imaginations and inner resources, they maintained a positive direction for themselves and their families during hard times.

How To Be Flexible and Adaptable

People with survivor personalities are flexible and adaptable. They have many ways of reacting to situations.

Before reading further about the survivor personality, take a moment to look at the list below and check any traits that you possess. Add any not listed in the blank spaces at the end.

—— tough	—— sensitive	—— messy	—— neat
—— gentle	—— strong	—— cooperative	—— rebellious
—— independent	—— dependent	—— lazy	—— hard-working
—— shy	—— bold	—— consistent	—— unpredictable
—— proud	—— humble	—— playful	—— serious
—— selfish	—— unselfish	—— pessimistic	—— optimistic
—— logical	—— creative	—— —————	—— —————

If your reaction to this short self-assessment was something like "I'm all of these!" then you are in very good shape. People with survivor personalities are paradoxical. They can be *both* one way and the opposite. They are serious and playful, selfish and unselfish, logical and creative.

Do you recognize this pattern? You have seen it in many places in the book. In Chapter 1, we described how *Student Success* is built on the principle that you can be both a good student and enjoy your college years to the fullest. You also read that students most likely to reach their goals are both optimistic and pessimistic about what lies ahead. Later, in the chapter on learning and teaching styles, we emphasized the value of being both "external" and "internal," both right-brained and left-brained, in adapting to various instructors.

People who can be only one way—such as serious but not playful—are greatly restricted in what they can do. Being one way but not the other is like having a car with no reverse gear. Paradoxical or counterbalanced pairs of personality traits make you flexible and give you control over what you do.

The list above is not intended to be complete. It is intended to make the point that the more pairs of paradoxical traits you acquire, then the more complex you are and thus the more successful you can be in dealing with any situation that develops.

The Playful Curiosity Habit

Being complex is not enough, however. In any difficult situation, it is essential to be very open to quickly assess and understand what is occurring. The capacity to quickly read, assess, and respond to what is occurring develops as a result of a lifetime of playful curiosity. It becomes a habit to ask such questions as:

How did they do that?
Why didn't this work?
Why did I do that?
I wonder why people do such things?
What would happen if . . . ?
What If I did the opposite from what people expect me to do?
How could I find out about . . . ?

This sort of curiosity gives a person much experience in dealing with unexpected developments, with stumbling into unknown circumstances, with being open to deal with bewildering situations. Survivors are drawn to the unusual, the complicated, and the mysterious. Thus, when a difficulty develops which you have not caused, the habit of being open to the new and unfamiliar predisposes you to quickly find out what is happening. Then, by being playful, you have much better control over the situation than you would have if you just felt helpless.

Things Working Well

People with survivor personalities need to have things working well. They have an above average need to get things working right. In reference to the Maslow hierarchy of needs, the need to have things working really well is described as a need for synergy and would be placed above self-actualization.

One consequence of this need for synergy is that people with survivor personalities are very good to have around. They have a knack for doing the little things that count. When some difficulty develops, they are "foul-weather friends." They show up to see what they can do to help out.

By combining selfishness and unselfishness in their way of life, they develop an attitude toward conflicts and problems that is best expressed as a question: "How can I interact with this so that things turn out well for all of us?"

In contrast, some people are oriented toward having things go wrong. They convert difficulties into the experience of being victimized. When problems develop, they respond to the circumstances in a way so that they can make people feel sorry for them and pity them for having such a tragedy occur.

Survivor habits and victim habits can become so deeply ingrained that people don't realize how much they make choices in responding to circumstances. Needing to have things work well is a part of being constantly open to looking for new and better solutions. Having things work well can mean giving up old assumptions and beliefs. Thus, another aspect of having a survivor personality is one of constantly asking questions to confirm how accurate your knowledge is. When better ways of perceiving or doing things comes along, people with survivor personalities adopt them.

Nonjudgmental Learning and Creativity

The ability to survive situations depends upon being able to read them accurately. Reading situations accurately results from having a nonjudgmental way of viewing the world. To be nonjudgmental is to absorb information about what exists. A judgmental attitude, on the other hand, means to quickly condemn or find something wrong at the first impression. Judgmental thinking is to quickly view things as right or wrong, to quickly think of people as being good or bad.

People who demonstrate judgmental thinking exhibit what psychologists call "premature perceptual closure." When someone begins to make a statement, the judgmental thinker is quick to decide what the statement is going to be and pass judgment on the statement. People who demonstrate judgmental thinking usually are described as having closed minds. They avoid empathy. They avoid learning how others view things. They translate much of what occurs in their world into simple categories and labels. Such thinking works directly contrary to good learning.

People with judgmental attitudes isolate themselves from accurate information about what is happening around them. You may recall that when you were a child your parents would ask you what you had been doing, and if you told them the truth, they would punish you or react in some very negative way. Most children learn that there are some things parents can't handle, and so children withhold infor-

166

mation from parents about what they are really doing, thinking, or feeling.

Regardless of how unpleasant the information is, there is much to be gained by learning how to appreciate being disillusioned. To view life as a school means that you can see human faults without becoming cynical. You discover that some students cheat during tests. You discover that the instructor doesn't catch the cheating or ignores it.

People with survivor personalities learn about the world without condemning it. They expect human beings to be human. They expect each human being to be unique and have an individual perspective. They absorb information about what exists just for the sake of knowing.

Research into creativity shows that people who score highest on creativity tests are people who are not judgmental. Individuals who score the lowest on tests of creativity are people who have strongly judgmental ways of thinking. To be creative is to come up with unusual ideas that work.

By understanding the relationship between nonjudgmental thinking and creativity, the survivor pattern becomes more clear. People with the survivor personality are very complex. You're never quite sure what they are going to do in any situation. Yet, because they read the situations quickly and accurately and have the intention of having things work out well, their solutions are often creative.

Hunches and Intuition

Associated with the quality of creativity is an awareness of subtle inner feelings. Sometimes survivors sense that something's wrong without knowing what it is. A tight stomach or an uneasy feeling can alert them. These feelings can be set off by anything, a person's tone of voice, something not said, a group's quietness, anything at all that doesn't fit.

In the classroom, someone with a survivor orientation will listen to what the instructor says and will also monitor whether or not the information being presented "feels right." If the information feels right, the survivor will absorb and make good use of it. On the other hand, if it doesn't feel right, there may be several alternatives, such as those we have described in earlier chapters. One of the alternatives is merely to take into account those things that the instructor believes are true, even if you don't believe that they are. Or you can speak up and challenge the instructor, based upon your own experience and your own view of things.

The ability to read and respond to subtle inner feelings gives survivors an ability to follow hunches. In general, women are better at this than men. Women are known for their intuition. This is no accident because women are usually raised with emotions as an important part of their lives.

Guided by Reason and Feeling

Survival often results from allowing oneself to be guided by feelings. A survivor's actions are not controlled by either emotions or logic. Survivors are influenced by both. There is a harmonious interaction between mind and emotions. With survivors, when emotions are likely to become disruptive, the objective mind can take over and maintain control. When one is more relaxed, survival may result from scanning one's emotions for clues as to what is right or wrong.

As we mentioned earlier, each of us has two brains. Survivors can use both the right brain and the left brain well. They can engage in nonverbal, emotional, musical, visual, intuitive, irrational, and metaphorical thinking. They can engage in logical and objective thinking. They are not limited to using only one way of thinking or the other.

Empathy for Others

The people who survive best in a variety of situations have good empathy for others. They can quickly "read" the emotional states, attitudes, and perceptions of others. They can step outside of their own feelings and perceptions to take into account the feelings and perceptions of others, even when disliked.

The empathy of survivors is not that of a weak, easily hurt "bleeding heart." It is more like the empathy of a defense attorney who must accurately understand the case against his or her client in order to prepare a good defense. Their empathy is not restricted to having a feeling for people who are experiencing difficulty or enjoyment. It includes having an understanding for people who live and think in disliked ways.

The attitude present in the empathy described here is "whether I enjoy you or dislike you, I am going to understand you as well as you understand yourself—and maybe even better." With this kind of empathy some survivors can be in such good control that they joke and play with their attackers.

Humor Makes the Difference

The ability to laugh and joke during a crisis is very practical. Laughing has a direct effect on one's ability to solve problems efficiently and deal with situations. Examples can be seen on television or in the movies. "Hawkeye" in the television series "M.A.S.H." is an excellent example. Writer Erma Bombeck reacts to events in her life with the humor typical of people with survivor personalities.

Why does humor help? Laughing reduces tension. Creative problem solving, accurate thinking, and good physical coordination are best in moderate emotional states. In athletics, the coach of a football team wants the linemen worked up to a high emotional state. In sports such as basketball, tennis, or baseball, a more moderate level of emotional arousal leads to better performance.

The humor used by survivors is directed toward the immediate situation. It is aimed at playing with the situation and poking fun at it. It is as though the person has the attitude "I am bigger than this situation. This is my toy. I am going to play with it."

The person seems to be asking, "How does this look from a different point of view? What would happen if I turned it upside down? What if the reverse were true? What unusual things exist here?" By playing with the situation and toying with it, the person keeps from being overwhelmed and at the same time is likely to come up with a way to survive.

It Isn't the Event, It's Your Reaction to It

People with survivor personalities rarely remain upset about what has been lost. They do not remain distressed when things have gone bad. They focus on the future. They know that nothing can be done now about what has happened. They accept responsibility for turning things around. They accept reality as it is. They accept responsibility for their reactions to conditions.

Martha Washington once said,

> "I am still determined to be cheerful and to be happy in whatever situation I may be—for I have also learned from experience that the greater part of our happiness or misery depends upon our dispositions and not upon our circumstances."

Be Responsible for Your Habits

As we stated at the beginning, this is a book about useful habits. Throughout the chapters, we've highlighted habits to develop—being responsible for yourself, using the SQ4R study steps, taking notes, using study schedules, preparing for tests, writing papers, and doing what successful students do.

Because a lack of friends can interfere with doing well in school, we included a chapter on ways to have more friends by developing habits that lead to good friendships.

Attitudes are habits. When necessary, we've shown how attitudes (mental and emotional habits) toward school, instructors, and life in general can help or hinder you. And now in this last chapter we've given attention to personality habits that can promote self-actualization and survival on your own by making life the best school of all.

Habits take time to develop, however. And you don't acquire habits by merely reading about them and thinking that certain ones would be nice to have. To have useful habits you need to devise a plan in which you consciously work at doing those things you wish to have occurring automatically.

Benjamin Franklin understood the importance of habits and in his autobiography tells of working to acquire good habits of character. He also understood it takes a long time to develop new habits. In the self-improvement plan that he devised for himself he worked on one habit at a time for one week at a time. He monitored his progress by using a checklist which he reviewed every night during his time for "reflections." Some fifty years later Franklin wrote about his habit plan, "On the whole, tho' I never arrived at the perfection I had been so ambitious of obtaining but fell far short of it, yet I was by the endeavor a better and a happier man than I otherwise should have been if I had not attempted it. . . ."

For a self-improvement plan to work you have to make it up for yourself. We recommend that you do what Franklin did. Make up a list of those behaviors and attitudes that you truly would like to acquire as habits. Write out a short behavioral description of each habit in practice. Set modest goals and expect to take years to reach them. Spend a few minutes each day recording how well you have done and reflect on your new experiences.

REMEMBER: The best investment you will ever make is in yourself. Are you ready to commence?

Self-Development Project: Developing a Talent for Serendipity

When people with survivor personalities talk about difficulties they've been through, they are likely to say, "I hated going through it, but it was the best thing that happened to me." Such a statement shows that the person learned so much from the experience that it truly was beneficial that they went through it. They reacted to life as a school and learned some valuable lessons about themselves and others. They were able to convert misfortune into good luck.

You can learn how to gain strength from adversity by discovering within you a talent for serendipity. The term "serendipity" was created by the English author Horace Walpole many years ago. He said that serendipity is a very special human capacity to turn an accident or unexpected difficulty into a good outcome through the use of wisdom. Serendipity is not merely having a lucky coincidence or discovery. Personal wisdom and effort must be elements that contribute to the good outcome.

To turn unpleasant difficulties into valuable learning experiences and convert misfortune into good luck, ask yourself serendipity questions such as:

170

"How can I interact with this so that things turn out well for all of us?"

"Why is it good for me that this happened?"

"What can I learn from this?"

"How might I turn this around and have everything turn out well?"

"What would be useful for me to do right now?"

"Is there an opportunity here that I never expected to have?"

"The next time something like this happens what will I do?"

"What is amusing about this?"

Questions such as these are the best way to organize your energies toward having things turn out well. By developing a talent for serendipity, you learn that when you are hit by adversity or misfortune you have a choice. You can dwell on your version of "If only other people would change, my life would be much better," or you can make things better for yourself.

Because you are a human being, you have an inborn capacity to learn what no one can teach you. To develop this talent, select a problem that you are trying to handle right now. Ask the serendipity questions and take your time looking for answers. Write the questions out in a diary if you like and talk with yourself about what answers you discover. By doing this, you may learn how to convert a major difficulty into the best thing that ever happened to you!

ACKNOWLEDGMENTS

There are many people to whom we owe much. . . .

Beverly Walter, and Jane Abbott, who through their enthusiasm, wit, and warmth have created a world that makes writing a pleasure.

James V. McConnell, who has bent over backward to share his love of writing and his many talents as a scholar and teacher.

Rowena Wilhelm, Director of the University of Michigan Reading and Learning Skills Center, whose support of our research and writing endeavors is greatly appreciated.

Donald E. P. Smith, whose earlier research continues to inspire us.

George Hoey, Glenn "Bo" Schembechler, and Donald Canham of the University of Michigan Athletic Department, whose recent support has provided us with a wealth of opportunities to learn more about the world of students.

John Gardner of the University of South Carolina, whose insights into the world of college orientation courses have been invaluable.

Ray Ashton, John Michel, Dan Loch, Nedah Abbott, Melanie Miller, and Susie Aitken of Holt, Rinehart and Winston, who have contributed so much to our publishing and editorial needs.

Lewis H. Walter, who could not wait to see the third edition of *Student Success*, and our mothers, who for some strange reason, continue to be proud of their sons.

Feedback Request

Do you have any study tips, comments, constructive criticism, or suggestions you would like to pass along to us? If so, please send them to us c/o:

Psychology Editor
College Department
Holt, Rinehart and Winston
383 Madison Avenue
New York, NY 10017

What did you find of most value in this book?

In what ways might it be improved?

Other comments:

HOUR	Sunday	Monday	Tuesday	Wednesday	Thursday	Friday	Saturday
7—8							
8—9							
9—10							
10—11							
11—12							
12—1							
1—2							
2—3							
3—4							
4—5							
5—6							
6—7							
7—8							
8—9							
9—10							
10—11							
11—12							

HOUR	Sunday	Monday	Tuesday	Wednesday	Thursday	Friday	Saturday
7–8							
8–9							
9–10							
10–11							
11–12							
12–1							
1–2							
2–3							
3–4							
4–5							
5–6							
6–7							
7–8							
8–9							
9–10							
10–11							
11–12							

HOUR	Sunday	Monday	Tuesday	Wednesday	Thursday	Friday	Saturday
7–8							
8–9							
9–10							
10–11							
11–12							
12–1							
1–2							
2–3							
3–4							
4–5							
5–6							
6–7							
7–8							
8–9							
9–10							
10–11							
11–12							

HOUR	Sunday	Monday	Tuesday	Wednesday	Thursday	Friday	Saturday
7—8							
8—9							
9—10							
10—11							
11—12							
12—1							
1—2							
2—3							
3—4							
4—5							
5—6							
6—7							
7—8							
8—9							
9—10							
10—11							
11—12							